What the House Holds

A Memoir of Loving a Child You Cannot Save

Brett Holloway

This is a work of memoir. The events and experiences described are based on the author's memories and contemporaneous documentation. All names have been changed or omitted to protect the privacy of individuals. The child at the center of this account is referred to throughout by the pseudonym Riley.

ISBN 979-8-9954005-1-6

First Edition, 2026

Published by Eshom Cabin Press

Printed in the United States of America

Contents

Author's Note

This story is true.

Every event described in these pages happened. Every conversation, every scene, I have reconstructed from memory and from the contemporaneous documentation I have kept over years: incident reports, written statements, video recordings, IEP documents, police reports, and the notes I made on my phone at two in the morning because I knew that if I didn't write it down, no one would believe me in the morning.

I have invented nothing. I have changed and excluded only names to protect the privacy of individuals. The child at the center of this account is my daughter.

She is fourteen years old. She has a documented history of severe early childhood trauma and carries diagnoses that include Reactive Attachment Disorder, Post-Traumatic Stress Disorder, Schizoaffective Disorder Bipolar Type, Intellectual Disability, Attention-Deficit/Hyperactivity Disorder combined type, and significant dissociative symptoms that are still being evaluated for an Identity Disorder. She has been violent toward every member of our family. She has poisoned me. She has made false allegations of abuse that triggered CPS investigations on multiple occasions. She has a part of herself she calls another person, who is not my daughter, who is demonstrably more intelligent than my daughter, and who frightens me in ways I did not know I was capable of being frightened.

I loved her before I knew her. I am still trying to love her now that I do. This is not a book about not loving her. It is a book about what love requires when love is not enough, when it is necessary but insufficient, when it is the beginning and not the end of the story.

I write with an educational background that gives me some clinical insight and vocabulary that most parents in this situation don't have. That has been both useful and isolating. I know what to call things. I know why they happen. I understand the neurobiology, the attachment theory, the diagnostic criteria. None of that knowledge has changed what happens in my house. But it has allowed me to document it with a precision that I hope makes these pages useful not only to parents who recognize their own lives here, but to clinicians who may have never seen what a home like mine actually looks like from the inside.

If you are a parent living what I am living, this book is for you first. You are not crazy. You are not failing. You are not alone. What is happening in your house is real, and the reason no one believes you is the same reason I had to start documenting everything: because some things are only credible when there is no other explanation left.

This book is also for my daughter, if she ever reads it; not as an accusation but as a record. As proof that she was seen, fully and honestly, even when the seeing was terrible.

CHAPTER ONE
Before

We are formed by what we cannot remember.

There is a version of this story that begins with hope, and I want to honor that version even as I tell the harder one, because both are true and neither cancels the other.

We chose adoption. My spouse Shane and I wanted a family. We reached out to the state foster care system and opened our home to children who needed a family, knowing full well what that meant, that children who enter the foster and adoption system do not come from easy circumstances, that early childhood trauma reshapes the developing brain in ways that are lasting and complex, that the children most in need of permanency are often the children hardest to parent. We are not people who romanticized the process. We had read the literature. We had completed the training. We had asked the hard questions. We knew this would be difficult. Well, we thought we knew.

We had already adopted her older brother a few years earlier, and believed we had learned how tough things could get.

We knew there were siblings out there, children our son had been separated from years earlier, children he had missed in the particular quiet way that kids carry grief they don't have language for yet. He asked about them sometimes. Not constantly, not dramatically. Just occasionally, the way you check a wound. And at some point he asked us directly: if there was ever a chance to adopt his siblings, would we?

We made him a promise that we would do everything in our power to bring them back together if that chance ever came.

I spent countless nights after that thinking about those kids. Worrying about their safety. Wondering what had happened to them. I had dreams about them. And finally, one day, I had to know. I called the DA and asked a simple question: if his siblings ever came back into state custody, would we be notified?

There was a pause. Then she said: they actually are in custody right now. But there's a situation.

We found out that not only were the two siblings we already knew about back in state custody, but there were now three additional children who had also been removed. Five kids, total. A situation, she had called it. I would have called it a door opening.

We didn't hesitate. We said yes before she finished talking.

• • •

The first family visit with her was set up at a roller skating rink. Neutral ground, something fun, a way to let the kids just be kids for a few hours before any of the heavier conversations about transitions and timelines had to happen. We loaded up a duffel bag the night before. I don't mean we threw a few things together. I mean we packed with intention. We bought clothes, toys, girly things we had picked out carefully, thinking about who she might be and what might make her feel seen. There was a puffy winter coat with a faux-fur lining. A light pink velvet overnight bag. Things that said: we thought about you. We picked these out for you specifically. We wanted you to know you were coming to a place where someone had already been imagining you.

We met in the parking lot. The CASA worker was there. And then there she was: a spunky little girl, hyperactive, all energy, taking in everything at once. The moment she saw the duffel bag she was interested. The moment she understood it was for her, something lit up in her face that I have thought about many times since. She was excited. She could not wait. She didn't wait. She pulled out that coat right there in the parking lot and put it on, grinning, not caring that it was not yet cold enough to need it. She wore it inside.

Our son's face when he saw his siblings all together again is something I will carry for the rest of my life. He had been scared for them since they parted ways. He had been carrying that fear quietly for years, the way kids carry things they've been told, implicitly or explicitly, that there is nothing to be done about. Watching him hug his sister for the first time in years, that was the version of this story that begins with hope. That moment was real.

• • •

The transition unfolded over the following months the way those plans do: short visits, then overnight stays, then weekends, the slow and structured process by which a foster child becomes yours. In the meantime, my mother and I spent a week in the humid heat of a Midwest summer working on her room. We found antique furniture and refinished every piece. Stripped it, rebuilt it, painted it. Hot pink and light pink, white and gold. A room that was not childishly princess but genuinely, extravagantly royal, the kind of room you see in magazines and think, someone made that for someone they loved. The CASA worker saw it. The caseworker saw it. Both of them said, only half joking, that they were jealous.

She loved it. Of course she loved it. And I loved that she loved it, because I had wanted her to walk into that room and understand, before a single word was spoken, that she was wanted here. That we had been waiting for her. That her family, us, had spent a week in the heat building her something beautiful.

I did not know, then, what the room would eventually look like after the rages. I did not know about the holes in the walls, the broken furniture, the locks on the doors. I did not know about any of it. All I knew was that a little girl, my son's sister, my little girl, was standing in a doorway looking at a pink and gold room, she was safe, and she was smiling, and so was I.

• • •

I will call her by her pseudonym throughout this book: Riley. She came to us in late 2019, shortly after two of her biological brothers who were also transitioning into our home. She was eight years old. Small for her age. Dark-eyed and watchful. What wasn't immediately apparent was that it was not the cautious watchfulness of a shy child in a new environment, but something more systematic, more deliberate. She was cataloguing us. Calculating. Deciding things. What those things were, it would take years to understand.

Her biological family had seventeen children. All seventeen were either removed by the state due to severe abuse and neglect, aged out, or in jail. I have reviewed what documentation exists. I will not reproduce the details here. What I will say is that whatever happened to Riley in the first years of her life was severe, sufficient to alter the fundamental architecture of how she relates to other people, how she understands safety and danger, how she interprets the intentions of the adults around her, and what she believes herself to be capable of and entitled to do.

None of that was visible to the naked eye when she walked through our door. She looked like a child. She acted like a child, or she acted like something close enough to a child that we filed the discrepancies under 'adjustment period' and 'trauma response' and kept going.

The adjustment period never ended. That is the thing about some children that no one tells you until you are years in: the window you are waiting for, the window in which the trust builds and the behaviors stabilize and the child begins to feel safe and responds to safety by becoming safer, does not always open. For some children, what looks like an adjustment period is simply the permanent condition. Not because they are broken. Not because they are bad. But because what was done to them was done before they had words or memories or any way to process it, and it lives in the body, not the mind, and the body does not negotiate.

We did see behavioral issues right away. But we weren't alarmed, not then. Given the trauma history, the years without consistent therapy or medication management, the upheaval of transitioning into a new home, what we saw seemed to fit within the range of what we expected. Tantrums. Defiance. Testing limits with an intensity that could be exhausting. We had seen it before. We had gone through the same kind of thing with her older brother when we brought him home, and he had settled over time. We had every reason to believe the same process would unfold with Riley. We were patient. We were consistent. We were, in retrospect, looking at the early chapters of something we did not yet have a name for, and reading them as something familiar.

• • •

In the beginning, I told myself a story about progress. Parents of traumatized children are told to measure in months, not weeks; in years, not months. I measured. I kept notes. I looked for the incremental improvements that the attachment therapist said would come. And there were some. There were flickers of genuine warmth and moments of real connection and days when Riley looked at me across a room with something in her eyes that I wanted to call love, and maybe it actually was.

What I was slower to see was the ceiling. Most children, given enough time and stability, make meaningful upward progress. The ceiling is high, even for children with significant early trauma. The arc bends. Things get better, slowly and imperfectly, but better.

Riley's arc did not bend in that direction. It bent in the other one. And the longer I kept trying to file the evidence under 'adjustment period,' the more evidence accumulated that what I was watching was not an adjustment at all. It was a revelation. The child I had brought home was showing me, gradually and then all at once, who she actually was, not who trauma had temporarily made her, but who she was in a way that might be permanent, or at least enduring enough that no timeline I could construct would account for it.

That realization came over years, not in a single moment. I do not think there is a single moment, in most cases like ours. There is a slow accumulation of evidence that eventually tips past the threshold of denial. Then there is the morning after the tipping, the morning you wake up and you know what you know and you cannot un-know it, and you have to figure out how to keep loving someone who cannot understand love.

CHAPTER TWO

The Architecture of Survival

The body remembers what the mind cannot.
It stores the oldest wounds in the deepest places,
and no amount of love can reach that far down.

The parents who told me my child was choosing this were wrong. The clinicians who said she would stop if the consequences were right were wrong. The people who recommended I be firmer, warmer, more consistent, more patient were wrong, not because those things do not matter, but because what they were describing is a child who can be reached by those approaches, and Riley cannot. What happened to her happened before she had words for it, and it lives in a part of her that consequences do not reach and love cannot fully access. Here is why.

The human brain develops from the bottom up, from the brainstem outward to the cortex. The earliest-developing structures are those responsible for survival: arousal, threat detection, the regulation of basic bodily functions. These structures are shaped by experience during the first years of life in ways that are foundational. They establish the baseline settings of the nervous system, the default calibration of what is safe and what is dangerous.

A child who is raised in an environment of chronic unpredictable threat, where caregivers are simultaneously sources of comfort and danger, where safety is never reliable, develops a nervous system calibrated for a world that never stops being dangerous. The threat-detection system is tuned high and stays tuned high. The capacity for self-regulation is limited, because self-regulation is a skill that develops in the context of a caregiver who co-regulates with you, who helps you calm down, who models and teaches the biological process of returning from arousal to baseline. If that co-regulation was absent or inconsistent or actively harmful, the child grows up with a nervous system that can escalate but cannot de-escalate, that can respond to threat but cannot find its way back to calm.

I understood all of this in the abstract long before I understood it in practice. The theory made sense to me. What I was not prepared for was how little the theory would help me in the moment, and how the moments would announce themselves not in the settings I expected, but in the most ordinary ones, when my guard was down and I still believed we were the kind of family who could take a road trip.

• • •

We were still in the transition period when we got approval to take Riley on an overnight trip to a neighboring state to visit my family. It was early enough that we were still in the phase of cautious optimism, still measuring things in small wins. The boys were excited. Riley was excited, or what passed for excited at the time. There were no issues getting ready that morning, no resistance to the three-hour drive. She chattered on and off the whole way up, asked questions about who we were going to see, seemed genuinely energized by the novelty of it. I remember thinking, somewhere in that drive, that this was going to be a good day.

Shane was in the driver's seat. I was passenger. I remember glancing over at him somewhere around the state line and I gave him a look, that look we had already developed, the shorthand for: it seems okay today. We were still learning that 'seems okay' was not the same as okay. We were still learning a lot of things.

My family was already waiting inside the restaurant when we arrived. It was a busy truck-stop style place, the kind with a full dining room and a steady stream of people coming and going. We found our table, made introductions, settled in. I picked up the menu and started looking at options for the kids. The older boys were well past the age of kids' menus, they were pre-teens who could eat their weight in food and still be hungry.

Riley was different. She was a small eater, picky, and not particularly adventurous. She asked for chicken strips. The kids' menu had chicken strips. I ordered from the kids' menu without giving it a second thought.

That was the trigger. Though I want to be careful about that word, because what I have come to understand is that the trigger is rarely the cause. The cause was already in motion before I ever opened the menu.

When Riley realized I had ordered from the kids' menu rather than the regular one, she went still in the particular way that I would come to recognize over years as the gathering before the storm. She sulked in her chair. Her expression darkened. She started mumbling under her breath, shooting looks around the table. I recognized it as the beginning of something and tried to keep things calm, low-key, unremarkable. Sometimes that had worked. That day it did not.

When the food arrived, she shoved her plate away. Then louder: she wasn't a baby. She wasn't going to eat off a baby menu. The volume climbed. I talked to her quietly, tried to redirect, tried to make the food seem appealing and the situation seem manageable. She shoved the plate again, harder. Her drink went over. And then we were in it, fully, publicly, in a packed restaurant full of strangers with my entire extended family at the table watching.

I asked her to come outside with me. Calmly, more than once. She refused. She got louder. People at nearby tables were looking. I asked again. She refused again and doubled down, her voice rising to the level where there was no longer any question that the entire dining room could hear her. At that point I made the decision I would make dozens of times after that: I picked her up and carried her out, moving as quickly and quietly as I could toward the side door to limit the disruption.

The moment we were outside, she started screaming. Not crying, screaming. Screaming that I was hurting her. Screaming that I was going to hurt her. We were in a truck stop parking lot on a busy highway, and she was screaming it at the top of her lungs, and people were stopping. People were watching. A few were walking toward us to see what was happening to this child. I kept moving, kept my face neutral, kept my voice low, and got her to the truck.

I sat her down in the back seat. She kicked the windows. She kicked the seats. She kicked the center console. She screamed. I stood outside the truck and waited, because I had already learned that getting in with her when she was at that level made it worse, not better. I stood there in a parking lot, in full view of strangers who had no context for what they were looking at, and I waited for it to end.

It ended, eventually. It always ends. She calmed, agreed to come back inside, and we returned to the table. By then, everyone had finished eating. The meal was over. My family, who had waited months to meet her, who had come out to this restaurant specifically for this visit, had eaten without us and were getting ready to leave. We had driven three hours for a lunch that lasted, for us, about fifteen minutes.

We ended up cutting the trip short, and did not stay the night.

On the drive home I thought about what had just happened and tried to file it somewhere useful. Adjustment period. New environment. Overstimulation. First trip. There were enough explanatory categories available that I could make it fit inside something manageable. And some of those explanations were probably true. But somewhere in the back of my mind, something had shifted slightly. A small recalibration I didn't yet have words for. I filed it away and kept driving.

Shane didn't say much on the way home. He didn't need to. I think we were both doing the same quiet math.

• • •

This is what I was working with. Not a child who was choosing to be difficult. Not a child who needed firmer limits or more consistent consequences or better parenting, though all of those things mattered, and I tried to provide all of them. A child whose nervous system had been wired for a world that no longer existed, and that wiring was not accessible to cognitive intervention. I could not reason her out of it. I could not love her out of it. I could not consequence her out of it. The wiring was below the level at which any of those tools operate.

Understanding this did help me be more patient. It did not make me safer. It did not prevent the escalations. It did not stop the injuries. But it allowed me to face the reality of Riley's situation without collapsing into a story about whose fault it was, and that mattered in the long run. It helped me keep trying.

• • •

Reactive Attachment Disorder is a diagnosis that clinicians give to children whose early caregiving environment was so deficient or dangerous that the normal attachment system failed to develop. Attachment is not a feeling. It is a biological system, a set of behaviors and internal working models that organize a child's relationship to caregivers and to the world. When that system does not develop normally, the consequences reach into every domain of functioning: emotional regulation, social cognition, the capacity for trust and intimacy, the ability to use relationships for comfort and support.

Children with RAD are often described as charming with strangers and difficult with primary caregivers. This is accurate, and it is also one of the most isolating features of parenting a child with this diagnosis. The child who terrifies you at home is often the child who impresses teachers, delights neighbors, and charms clinicians. The disparity is not accidental. It reflects the architecture of the disorder: primary caregivers represent the attachment system that failed, and that failure is re-enacted in every close relationship. Strangers are safe precisely because they are not close, not yet, not enough to trigger the mechanisms that govern intimate bonds.

I have sat in meetings with clinicians who had just spent forty-five minutes with Riley and were telling me how well she was doing, and I have had to explain, carefully, with precise documentation, because without documentation it sounds like the defensive complaint of an overwhelmed parent, that what they observed in their office is not what I observe in my home. This is not a criticism of those clinicians. They saw what they saw, and what they saw was real. It is simply not the whole picture. The whole picture requires years of proximity, and I am one of a small number of people who have spent that time close enough to see it.

There is a fifth diagnosis in her record that I want to name here, because it compounds every item on the list above in ways that matter to anyone trying to understand what I am describing. Attention-Deficit/Hyperactivity Disorder, combined presentation, moderate severity, formally confirmed by psychological evaluation. The impulsivity that ADHD produces, the inability to inhibit a response already in motion, the attention dysregulation that makes sustained self-monitoring functionally impossible: these are not choices or failures of effort. They are documented deficits in executive function. They interact with the fear-based nervous system wiring in ways that strip away whatever modulation might otherwise exist. Understanding RAD, PTSD, and Schizoaffective Disorder together without accounting for ADHD is like trying to understand a fire without accounting for the accelerant.

That trip was, by the standards of what was coming, extremely minor. I know that now. At the time it felt significant. And it was significant, not because of what it was, but because of what it was the beginning of. Every family has an early story like that one, the first time something tipped and the situation got away from them in public, or in front of people they loved. Most families don't have hundreds and hundreds more after it. We did. That afternoon in the parking lot was the first chapter of a very long book, and I was still, at that point, under the impression that I was reading a short story.

CHAPTER THREE
What Home Becomes

You stop calling it vigilance when it becomes the only thing you know how to do.

There is a process by which a family reorganizes itself around a child's illness, and it happens so gradually that you do not notice it until you surface from the process and look around at the life you are living and realize that everything in it has been shaped by the management of one person's symptoms. Everyone's entire existence in the home revolves around fear. When will the next issue arise? Who is at risk?

Our home is locked up in ways that homes are not ordinarily locked. Not against intruders, but against an internal threat. The knives are locked. The cleaning supplies are locked. The scissors are locked; pens, pencils. The medications are locked. I have sometimes stood in my own kitchen, cooking dinner, and thought: this is what it looks like to prepare a meal in a prison. I do not have the staffing of a prison. I do not have shift changes or incident documentation infrastructure or a clinical supervisor on call. I have locked drawers, locked cabinets, biometric locks on bedrooms, a phone full of video recordings, and a spouse who is as exhausted as I am.

The schedule of our house is built around Riley. Not because we have no other priorities, we do, we work, we own a business, we have three other children. The schedule is built around Riley because the consequences of failing to structure her environment appropriately are severe enough that they override every other consideration. We cannot leave for a spontaneous errand without planning supervision. We cannot have guests come to our home without briefing them. We cannot have a conversation in another room without one ear tuned toward wherever she is. This is not paranoia. It is learned pattern recognition. We have learned what happens when attention lapses. We do not allow attention to lapse.

We wake already in a state of assessment, before anyone has spoken, we are reading the baseline. What did the night bring? Is she in her Riley state this morning, or is she somewhere else? The question of 'somewhere else' will require its own chapter. For now: the morning begins with assessment, because the shape of the morning usually determines what kind of day we are going to have.

Hygiene is a site of persistent conflict. This sounds, when I say it aloud to people outside my life, like an ordinary parenting complaint. Teenagers resist hygiene. Kids forget to brush their teeth. I understand why people hear it that way. What they cannot see from the outside is the quality of the resistance, the deliberate, systematic nature of it, the way she waits to see what I will do, the way she escalates through her refusals in a pattern that is not random but organized. The refusal to bathe, to change clothes or brush teeth is not negligence. It is a performance of control. It is a message: this is mine, and you cannot have it.

The afternoon transition from school to home is the most reliably dangerous time of our day. She comes through the door already compressed, the structure of the school day has been holding her in one shape, and the moment she crosses the threshold, that shape releases. We have learned to give her minimal engagement. No instructions. No questions about the day. No corrections. Just presence: low-key, quiet, available. On a good day, this works. On a bad day, there is no protocol that helps. The escalation begins regardless, and our job shifts from prevention to containment.

Evenings are long. Bedtime is a process that takes two to three hours on ordinary nights and longer on hard ones. She does not self-regulate toward sleep. She self-regulates toward escalation. The later it gets, the louder she becomes, the more provocative, the more inclined toward self-injury. I have stood outside her bedroom door at midnight, listening to her bang her own head against the wall, and made the calculation, the terrible, ongoing calculation that parents in this situation make constantly, about when intervention helps and when it accelerates the behavior it is trying to stop.

That calculation has no clean answer. I have been wrong in both directions. There are nights when going in helps and nights when it feeds the escalation. The difference, when I can identify it, is often about which state she is in, but by the time I have identified which state she is in, the window for the right intervention has often passed.

• • •

Shane and I do not have evenings. We do not have weekends. We do not have date nights or spontaneous mornings or the ordinary rhythms of a couple's life. We have shifts. We have the management of a household that runs at crisis level more days than not, and we manage it together because neither of us can sustain it alone for more than a few hours.

There is something I want to put on record about Shane, because this account cannot be honest without it. Shane is the one who stays calm when I am running out of calm. He is physically present in the way that crisis demands, steady, consistent, not easily rattled. There was a night, somewhere in the second year, when Riley had been in a full rage for nearly three hours and I had reached the end of what I had. I walked out of the living room and into our bedroom and sat down on the edge of the bed and could not make myself stand back up. Shane came in a few minutes later, looked at me, and didn't say anything. He just went back out and took my place in the living room. That was it. That was the whole thing. He took the next shift without being asked and without making me feel like I had failed, and I have not forgotten it. In a situation where there is very little grace to go around, that moment was grace.

I do not write about our depletion out of self-pity, because self-pity is not useful and I do not have the energy for it. But I think it matters for the record: parents of children like ours are depleted in ways that are invisible to the outside. We do not look depleted. We show up to meetings and write coherent letters and maintain documentation and strongly fight and advocate within systems for our children. We look like people who are managing. We are managing. But management has a cost, and the cost compounds, and at some point, the point we have reached, the cost exceeds what body and mind can sustain.

• • •

There is one more thing that belongs in this chapter. The events I am about to describe sit at the intersection of what home becomes and what family trust costs when it is weaponized. I have placed the full account here, in the domestic chapter, because it is fundamentally a story about what happened inside our house: inside a therapy session, inside a backyard, inside a relationship I had tried to build with honesty and openness. The implications of it, the pattern it belongs to, I will return to in a later chapter. But the beginning of it belongs here.

The cameras went up after the first false allegation. I want to be precise about that timeline, because I have been asked, by well-meaning people, and once or twice by less well-meaning ones, whether the cameras represent a surveillance-oriented, punitive approach to parenting.

They do not. And the story of why they are there is one I have to tell carefully, because it involves something I disclosed to Riley in therapy under the assumption that trust and connection was being built. I was wrong about that.

Earlier in the week before the cameras went up, while in a therapy session, Riley and I had discussed her tendency to blame her past for her present behaviors. We talked about how people can be victims of things that happened to them and still choose not to let those things define them. I told her about my own childhood. I told her I had been abused. I told her I had grown up in a home that felt unsafe, and that I had been sexually abused as a child. I told her I had worked hard not to live in that victimhood, that I moved forward and did not dwell on what had happened. I thought this conversation was connecting. It seemed like we had reached each other on a level that was real.

What I had actually done was hand her a weapon.

A few days later, Riley was upset about being told no. What followed was hours of screaming and banging and hitting and scratching herself, alleging abuse by us as she injured herself. In a moment of exhaustion and frustration, I told her that she was not going to act like an animal in our house, and to go outside to the back yard if she was going to act like that.

Something shifted when she went outside. I could see it from the window. The tantrum was still going, but it was changing quality. She was calming, and calm during a major Riley event is not something to be excited about. Calm is not resolution. Calm is preparation.

I watched through the back door window as she continued to yell 'you're hurting me... you're abusive,' and then, as I stood there watching, she forcefully shoved her hands inside the front of her pants.

She was staging an injury. Staging physical evidence she later admitted she intended to use as a claim of sexual abuse against me. She was going to use what I had shared in therapy, something that had hurt me to the core as a child, as a weapon against me. She had listened to my disclosure and filed it away, not as a moment of connection, but as an asset.

I pulled out my phone and documented what I was seeing in real time. Because I already knew: without proof, her word would carry the weight of a child's word against parents, and that weight is not trivially distributed.

The cameras went up the next day. They are not a reflection of how I wish things were. They are the result of that afternoon, and of a pattern of behaviors that made them necessary. They protect our other children. They provide documentation we otherwise would have no corroboration for. And on the day my child stood in a backyard staging a false claim of sexual abuse against a parent who had just, days earlier, trusted her with the most painful truth of his own childhood, cameras became the only thing standing between our family and a lie that could have destroyed it.

I do not know how to describe what it feels like to realize that your love for a child is being weaponized against you. I am not sure there is language for it. What I can tell you is that after that afternoon, something changed in the way I understood what we were dealing with. Not my love for her, at least I don't think. But my understanding of what I was facing. Some things, once you have seen them, you cannot un-see. And once you have seen your child do that, you carry it differently from everything that came before.

CHAPTER FOUR

The Room

It started with the bedpost.

I described her room in the first chapter of this book, because it belongs there, in the version of this story that begins with hope. My mother and I had spent a week in the heat of a Midwest summer building it. Antique furniture, stripped and refinished by hand. Hot pink and light pink, white and gold. A room that looked like someone had thought carefully about who this little girl was and what she deserved. Riley had walked through that door and her face did the thing I had been hoping for. That room was real. That moment was real.

What I want to describe now is what happened to that room over the years that followed, because the room is a record in its own right, and the record is worth keeping.

• • •

It did not happen all at once. That is the first thing to understand. If it had happened all at once it would have been easier to name and respond to. What happened instead was incremental: a bedpost broken here, a blanket destroyed there. A toy taken apart. A book shredded. A piece of clothing ruined in a way that was not accidental. Each individual incident was explainable, or at least containable within an explanation. Children break things. Children with trauma histories sometimes destroy things as a form of communication or dysregulation. We replaced what was broken. We addressed the behavior in therapy. We kept going.

The princess room went first: the decorations, the carefully chosen furniture, the things we had refinished by hand. Then the replacement items. Then the next round of replacements. Over time, in response to the destruction of things that mattered, we stripped the room down to what we thought was the essential minimum: a bed, a dresser, clothes, a small number of toys and books. We were trying to reduce the losses. We were trying to give her less to destroy. What we were actually doing, though we did not understand this yet, was moving through the phases of a process that had its own destination, and we had not yet seen where it was going.

She destroyed the simplified room too. The bed. The dresser. The remaining toys and books. The clothing.

All of it, eventually, in one way or another, was gone. And then, with nothing left to destroy, the behavior shifted into something else.

• • •

We did a weekly room safety sweep. We had learned to do this carefully and without announcement, because the purpose was not punitive but protective: to remove sharps, to identify hazards, to document what was there and what was not. We did not typically go through her bedding or drawers. Over the previous few sweeps we had been noticing a smell we could not locate. On this one, I pulled back her blanket, and the smell reached me before I fully understood what I was looking at.

The blanket was coated in areas. Feces, urine, menstrual blood: layered, dried, layered again. The pillow was soaked through with urine. The mattress had absorbed so much that it was wet through. The dresser drawers held used menstrual pads, stuffed in among clothing that had been urinated and defecated on and then folded and put away as if it were clean. The smell in that room, once the blanket was lifted, was the smell of something that had been happening for a long time in an enclosed space. It was not a smell I had encountered before. It is not a smell I have been able to forget.

We threw away the mattress. We threw away the pillow. We threw away nearly all of the clothing. We replaced everything. We addressed the behavior in therapy hoping it would stop. She continued doing it.

• • •

The hygiene refusals I described in an earlier chapter are not separate from this. They are part of the same system. The refusal to bathe, to change clothes, to brush teeth: these are not negligence or forgetting. They are intentional. The soiled clothes she would attempt to wear to school, arguing they were clean, arguing the visible stain was something else, arguing in the face of direct sensory evidence that there was nothing wrong with what she was wearing. The deliberateness of the denial was as striking as the behavior itself.

On one occasion she came downstairs with feces visibly on her clothing. I asked her about it directly. She denied it. I insisted she change. She refused, and then she argued: it was chocolate. She went further than that to make her point. She licked it.

It was not chocolate.

She knew it was not chocolate. She did it anyway, with the same flat certainty she brings to every denial, the same quality of assertion that does not bend under the weight of direct evidence because for her, at that moment, the assertion was the point. Not the truth of it. The assertion.

• • •

The menstrual hygiene piece requires its own accounting, because it is distinct and because it is the part that most required us to adapt in ways I had not anticipated having to adapt. She knows how and when to use menstrual pads. She has been taught. She is capable of it. She is not embarrassed of it. The refusal is not a knowledge deficit. She refuses to use them, or uses them and refuses to change them appropriately, and with either, the result is that she bleeds through her clothing. She will sit across from you, actively bleeding through her clothes, and deny that she is on her period. She will argue, with complete composure, that she is not bleeding.

She has come downstairs in blood soiled clothing and denied it. She has attempted to go to school that way.

One morning she came downstairs covered in blood. Not a small amount. She had taken used menstrual pads and wiped them across herself: her face, her arms, her hands, her legs. She stood in front of us and denied it. The denial in that moment was not confusion or dissociation. It had the same quality as all the other denials: flat, immediate, sustained. She looked at what she had done to herself and said it was not what it was.

We have worked on this in therapy. We have worked on it consistently, across multiple therapists, over years. The behavior has not changed in response to therapeutic intervention. It has continued, modified only by the structural adaptations we have made to the environment: her clothing and menstrual supplies are now kept downstairs and checked in and out. She has access to what she needs; it is just no longer stored in her room unsupervised.

• • •

Her room now contains a waterproof mattress. Stain resistant sheets, a waterproof pillow, a single blanket. There are no decorations. There are no books on a shelf or toys in a bin or clothes in a dresser. There is nothing in that room that can be meaningfully destroyed, because everything that could be has been. The pink and gold room that my mother and I built in a week of summer heat is gone so completely that I sometimes have difficulty believing it existed. The room it has become is not a punishment. It is the result of a process that moved in one direction over years, and stopped where it stopped because we ran out of things to replace.

I think about the room we built sometimes. Not often, because there is not enough time in the day for that kind of thinking, but sometimes. The way she looked standing in that doorway with her face doing the thing I had hoped for. I built that room for a child I believed was going to grow into it. The room she has now is the room the years produced. Funny how it is still the same room.

CHAPTER FIVE

The Rages

There is no vocabulary adequate to the middle of it. Language only comes back after.

I have read clinical descriptions of severe emotional dysregulation in children with complex trauma histories. I have used that language myself, in documentation and in letters to providers. But I want to try, in this chapter, to move past the clinical language and describe what a rage actually looks, sounds, and feels like when it is happening in a home with other people in it.

The onset is rarely explosive. That is the first thing to understand. The explosion is preceded by a gathering, a change in the quality of the air in the room. Her eyes shift. Multiple people have described this independently, and I want to be clear that I am not the only one who has seen it: the darkness in her eyes that precedes a significant escalation. Her teacher documented it in writing. School staff who barely knew her documented it after a single incident. A family friend who met her at a gathering noticed it before anything happened. The eyes go darker, the expression flattens, the body language changes. There is a stillness that is not calm. It is the stillness of something coiling.

Then there is a trigger. The trigger is often trivial, a correction, a redirection, a reminder about hygiene or rules or bedtime routines. Sometimes there is no identifiable trigger. The escalation begins regardless, as if it had been decided before the triggering event rather than caused by it. I have come to believe that the trigger is often incidental, that the escalation was already in motion at a neurological level by the time any external event occurred, and the external event is simply the first available explanation rather than the actual cause.

Once it begins: screaming. Long, sustained, high-volume screaming that is not crying. It is not the sound of a child in pain or grief. It is something more like a siren: flat affect, enormous volume, relentless. Interspersed with profanity, with threats, with statements about what she is going to do to herself and to us. She punches walls. She slams doors hard enough that we have had to replace door frames. She throws whatever is within reach. She has slammed into walls and windows with her own body, with her fists, with her elbows.

The self-injury during rages is the part that is hardest to describe without sounding like I am exaggerating, so let me be specific and let the specificity speak for itself. I have documented the following, over and over, in real time: kicking walls, punching and elbowing windows, slamming her body into the staircase repeatedly, head-banging on both the stairs and the windows, throwing herself backward onto the edges of the stair steps so they struck her head and neck, twisting her neck forcefully and laterally, bending her fingers backward at the joints, bending her toes backward, punching her own thighs and shins, bending her ankles sideways, scratching her arms and face, ripping and tearing clothes apart with her hands and teeth. I have video of this. I documented it in writing as it happened because I knew, from experience, that descriptions without documentation are not believed in the way that documentation demands belief.

The standard model of emotional dysregulation involves escalation, a peak, and then de-escalation. The arc rises and falls. With Riley, the arc does not fall in the expected way. She escalates, appears to approach a peak, and then re-escalates. The four-plus-hour episodes are not four hours of sustained maximum intensity, they are four hours of escalation, partial reduction, re-escalation, partial reduction, re-escalation, in a cycle that does not follow the ordinary rules of emotional regulation because the ordinary rules require a nervous system that can self-regulate, and hers cannot.

• • •

One of the most unsettling features of the rages is what comes after. There is a settling. An abrupt one that I cannot fully account for and that never stops being jarring. The screaming stops. The body stills. The eyes clear, or change, or do something that is the opposite of what they were doing twenty minutes earlier. And she moves on. Not in the way a child who has had a tantrum and recovered moves on, not with the residue of the episode visible in her face or her behavior, but with something closer to a clean slate. The incident is often not accessible to her afterward. She denies it or misremembers it or frames it in ways that bear no resemblance to what was documented on video just moments before. This is not lying in the ordinary sense. It reflects something about how the incident was processed, or not processed, during the episode itself.

The aftermath for the rest of us is different. Shane and I, our other children, do not clean slate. We carry the event in our bodies, in our nervous systems, in the accumulated residue of thousands of episodes over years. Our older sons carry it. Our youngest carries it, even though he is seven and cannot fully articulate what he is carrying. And we are expected, every time, to re-engage as if it has ended for everyone, because the alternative is to remain in the aftermath indefinitely, and we cannot afford that. There are other children. There is a next hour. There is life we have to continue.

The episode ends for Riley. For everyone else in the house, it does not end. It accumulates in the body, in the nervous system, in the weight of knowing it will happen again.

CHAPTER SIX
Aubrey (aka The Mean Girl)

She has a name for the part of herself she does not claim.

I do not know how to write this chapter without sounding like I am describing something from a film rather than from my living room. I am going to try to be as precise and grounded as I know how to be, and I am going to ask the reader to hold that alongside the lived reality, because both are necessary and neither is sufficient alone.

My daughter has an alter, and her name is Aubrey.

I first encountered her just under a year after Riley moved in with us. Riley was in third grade. The behavioral issues had continued to escalate through that first year: tantrums every other day or so, increasing reclusiveness, more and more time spent alone in her room. We were doing PCIT therapy at the time, trying to address attachment-related issues. We had cameras installed throughout the house by then, not yet fully understanding everything they would eventually document.

What we had started to notice was harder to name than a tantrum. When Riley was upset, she was now acting differently, and there was a quality to the difference that did not feel like a mood shift. It felt like something else. When she was in her room she would talk to herself: not the quiet self-talk of a child working through a problem, but full exchanges, arguments, sometimes shouting at no one. We started finding notes she had written to people who didn't exist, and the notes were not all in the same hand. Some were in her usual writing: rounded, bubbly, girlish. Others were aggressive and cramped, hard-pressed into the paper, the letters leaning differently. Not the same child's handwriting. Different enough that we kept them.

And then there were the eyes. My mother was the first one to name it clearly. She said: it looks like her eyes just go dark. Like there's nothing there, just darkness. Once she said that, I knew exactly what she meant, because I had seen it too and had not had words for it. The eyes would change before the behavior changed. Not a subtle shift in expression; something more total than that. Pupils dark and wide, looking straight through you rather than at you.

Riley had been caught stealing food again the night we first met the alter. Riley stole constantly and compulsively: small things, food especially. We would find hoarded wrappers, rotten food tucked into corners of her room, evidence of a child who had learned very early that food was not reliable and had never fully unlearned it. When we confronted her about it that night, she lost control. And as she did, I watched it happen in real time for the first time. I saw the change in her eyes as it occurred, not after the fact, not in a photograph or on a recording, but live, while I was standing right there. The pupils expanded. The focus shifted. She looked through me in a way that made the back of my neck go cold, and what came out of her after, the pure hatred in how she spoke, did not sound like the child I had put to bed the night before.

I cannot tell you exactly how we arrived at the name 'the mean girl,' because those early months run together the way that relentless things do. What I do know is that Riley's third-grade teacher named it before I did in any formal way. She had reached out to me about an incident at school. Riley had been refused access to the Chromebook, and the teacher had noticed the change: the eyes, the posture, the shift in affect. She did something instinctive. She looked at Riley and said: I want to talk to Riley. The child in front of her said no. Then said: I'm the mean girl.

The teacher told me later that she thought she had made a mistake by calling it out. The rest of that day had been bad in ways that seemed directed specifically at her. The next morning the school called. Riley had reported that the teacher had locked her in a closet for the entire previous day. She had not. The teacher had made the mean girl visible, and the mean girl did not like to be seen. The allegation was the response.

A few weeks later, at bedtime, we learned her actual name.

Riley had been difficult all day, one of those grinding, accumulating days where nothing is a catastrophe but everything is a friction. By evening she had lost her dessert as a consequence while her brothers ate theirs. The battle that followed was full-scale: screaming, stomping, scratching her own arms and face, accusations that she was being starved. Her eyes had changed. She was the mean girl, clearly and completely, and I was done pretending otherwise. I looked at her and said it directly: I'm tired of dealing with the mean girl. I want to talk to Riley.

She stopped. Looked at me with an expression I had not seen before. Not rage, not contempt; something almost offended. Corrective.

'I'm not the mean girl. I'm Aubrey.'

And that was that. She had a name. She had always had a name. We just hadn't known to ask for it.

• • •

Since that night, we have had hundreds of interactions with this alternate presentation. I use that clinical language deliberately, because the phenomenon is real and documented and has been independently corroborated by multiple people who have no reason to coordinate with each other in fabricating it. Riley's school counselor asked her, during one of these episodes, whether the counselor was even speaking with Riley. The response was direct: 'No, you're fucking not.' She had been non-responsive to the name Riley and turned immediately when addressed as Aubrey.

Let me describe the differences between the two presentations, because the differences are not subtle and they are not explicable as ordinary behavioral variation or oppositional behavior.

Riley has a documented Full Scale IQ of 54. She reads at approximately a second-grade level. Her academic functioning is consistently assessed as significantly below age expectations across all domains. Her executive functioning is impaired. She has difficulty with planning, sequencing, and task completion. These are not character traits. They are documented cognitive findings from formal evaluations conducted by licensed psychologists.

Aubrey does not function at that level. Aubrey plans. Aubrey anticipates. Aubrey completes tasks that Riley, at her documented cognitive level, should not be able to complete. This is not a matter of motivation or effort. Oppositionality does not raise IQ. A child who is cognitively incapable of something does not become capable of it simply because she wants to. The differential is real. Her handwriting changes, we have the notes to prove it, kept over years, in two distinct hands from what is supposed to be the same child. Her vocabulary changes. Her sentence structure changes. Her reasoning changes. Whatever is happening when Aubrey is present is happening at a cognitive level that is measurably different from Riley's documented baseline.

The physical changes are equally well-documented. Multiple school staff, her counselor, her classroom teachers, her paraprofessionals, her principal, all independently documented observable changes during what appear to be dissociative states: pupil dilation, voice changes (one staff member described the shift as moving from a 'more timid voice with soft timbre' to a voice that was 'loud, forceful, and had a dark timbre'), postural changes ('stood taller,' 'body stiffen and jerk'), and facial expression changes ('face looked different, hard; I could see malice'). One staff member noted that she could observe Riley's body 'ripple and relax' during transitions between states. These staff members were writing independently. They did not compare notes before producing their documentation. The convergence of their observations is clinically significant. It is also, for those of us who have been watching this for years, simply accurate.

• • •

Living with this is strange in ways that do not resolve over time. I have become familiar with the transitions. I can often read the signs of an impending shift before it happens. But familiarity has not made it less disorienting. There is the experience of looking at your child and not knowing who you are looking at. There is the experience of a conversation that begins in one presentation and shifts mid-sentence into another. There is the experience of watching her scream 'you're hurting me' while she is the one inflicting the injury, a dissociation so complete that she appeared genuinely not to know that the hands causing the pain were her own.

I want to be precise about my position here. I am not diagnosing my child. The dissociative symptoms are documented in psychological evaluations as requiring further clinical evaluation. The clinical picture is not settled. What I am doing in this chapter is describing what I observe, carefully and as specifically as I can. Whether the system ultimately classifies it as Dissociative Identity Disorder or as something else, the observable behavior is what it is, and the implications for how Riley thinks, plans, and acts are consequential regardless of what label is applied.

Aubrey concerns me more than Riley does, in certain respects. Riley at her most explosive is dangerous in a way that is visible and acute. Aubrey is dangerous in a different way: quietly, with planning, with intelligence, and without Riley's affect to signal that something is wrong. The poisoning incident, which I will describe in its own chapter, has the signature of Aubrey. The sophistication of the plan, the patience of the execution, the absence of agitation or distress, the calm matter-of-fact accounting of motive after the fact.

That is not Riley. That is something else.

Aubrey does not like to be seen. We learned that the hard way. We have been careful, since then, about when and how we acknowledge her directly. But we know she is there. She has always been there. She just finally had a name.

CHAPTER SEVEN

When Your Child Tries to Kill You

Some things cannot be called 'behaviors.'
Some things require a different word entirely.

We were out of state for the wedding of a childhood friend of mine. We had rented an Airbnb large enough for all six of us, a two-level house that split naturally along the lines we had learned to organize ourselves around: Shane took the lower level with the three boys, and I kept Riley with me on the upper level.

The second morning I started a cup of coffee. I do not usually drink coffee, I am an energy drink person, but we had not yet made it to a gas station and coffee was what the Airbnb had. It brewed too hot, hotter than I like, so I set it on the counter to cool and got pulled away by distraction. There were wedding logistics that needed attention, Shane needed help getting the boys up and ready on the lower level, and Riley was in the shower on the upper level. I went back and forth between the two floors, occupied, doing what you do on the morning before a wedding when you have four children and a schedule to keep.

I had set my drink on the counter to cool.

I had left my drink unattended.

When I came back and took a drink of the coffee, the pain was immediate. It felt the way I imagine drinking near-boiling water would feel: a searing across my tongue, the roof of my mouth, the back of my throat. I went straight to the sink and drank cold water. My mouth was throbbing. I threw the rest of the coffee out and told myself it had been much hotter than I thought.

As the day went on, the pain did not diminish the way a small burn does. My tongue and the roof of my mouth felt blistered. My throat had started to hurt in a way that reached deeper than a surface burn. By afternoon I found an urgent care. I told them I had burned my mouth on coffee. They looked at my mouth and throat, confirmed burns and blisters, and sent me home with a prescription for numbing lozenges I could not use because of a lidocaine allergy.

The next day was the wedding. There was no time to slow down. Shane had all four kids to manage through the ceremony and the reception, and I was there for my friend. By the end of the night my mouth had begun to peel. My tongue was cracking. My throat looked like I had strep and felt worse. My sinuses were dry and raw in a way that did not match any mouth burn I had experienced before.

The morning after the wedding I went back to urgent care. Bleeding had started: small cracks opening along my tongue, the blisters on the roof of my mouth enlarging, my throat increasingly raw. The provider examined me and then asked, carefully, whether I had done something to hurt myself. Whether I was suicidal. I was genuinely confused. I had been in two days ago for a coffee burn. Then they explained. What I had was not a thermal burn. What I had were chemical burns. They asked whether it was possible I had somehow ingested something caustic.

My mind went immediately to Riley.

This would not be the first time. She had attempted to put toilet bowl cleaner on my toothbrush in the past. I had found the toothbrush compromised, smelling of it, confronted her, and she had denied it with the same flat certainty she denied everything. That incident had never been fully resolved. I had no proof, only the physical evidence and a suspicion I had filed and carried forward. Sitting in an urgent care out of state being told I had chemical burns in my mouth, I did not have to work very hard to connect the dots.

We went back to the Airbnb and looked. Under the bathroom sink on the upper level, where Riley had been left alone in the shower while I was downstairs on the morning in question, we found a bottle of Drano. It was empty.

When we confronted her with the bottle she denied it, as she always does at first. Then, faced with the empty container and the burns in my mouth and the question that had no other answer, she admitted it. She had poured Drano into my coffee.

She said it without visible distress. Flat, factual, brief. She had done it. That was the fact.

• • •

Back home, in a session with her counselor, the incident was revisited. Her counselor asked her why she had done it. Riley's response was delivered without emotion, without agitation, without any of the affect that typically accompanies even the most alarming things she says.

'I wanted to watch him die.'

Just six words. No charge behind them. A statement of motive, offered the way you might tell someone why you ordered a particular thing off a menu.

My child put drain cleaner in my drink. I drank it and sustained chemical burns to my mouth and throat that required two urgent care visits and bled for days. When asked why, she said she wanted to watch me die. And then the session ended and she went to school and came home and had dinner with the family. As if nothing had ever happened.

• • •

On a separate occasion, at school, she placed soap into a teacher's coffee. That incident is documented in her educational and clinical records. Two incidents with the same methodology: identify a target, identify a beverage, introduce a substance, wait. A pattern has implications that a single incident does not.

The act of poisoning requires a specific kind of cognitive functioning: the ability to plan across time, to sequence steps, to execute without detection, to manage one's own affect during the execution so as not to signal intent. These are executive functions. Riley has a documented Full Scale IQ of 54 and documented impairment in executive functioning across multiple formal evaluations. She should not, on paper, be capable of this.

Which brings us back to Aubrey.

What I observe is that the poisoning does not have the signature of Riley's dysregulated, impulsive, escalating violence. It has a different signature entirely:

cold, patient, planned, interested in a specific outcome. Interested in watching. That quality of spectatorship in her stated motive is the part I find most clinically significant and most difficult to digest. She did not say she wanted to hurt me. She said she wanted to watch me die. The interest was in the observation of the outcome, not in an expression of rage.

I had chemical burns that took over two weeks to fully heal. I have a daughter who had tried to kill me.

CHAPTER EIGHT

The Allegation Machine

She learned before she had language that a good offense was the only defense.

There is a pattern, and once you see it you cannot unsee it. Riley makes a false allegation of abuse, neglect, or assault. She does this consistently, specifically, and in close proximity to a confrontation, a consequence, or a limit being set. The allegation is not random. It is targeted. And it is almost always accompanied by physical evidence she has staged herself.

She is not confused about what happened. She is not misinterpreting a situation or processing a memory inaccurately. She identifies a target, identifies a mechanism, and produces an allegation designed to shift attention from her behavior to ours. That is what I mean by the title of this chapter. It is a machine. It runs with consistency and intention and it produces predictable outputs.

The earliest allegations were about food. She was not being fed. She was being starved. This is a pattern that began early and has never fully stopped. She would eat dinner and forty minutes later claim she was starving. She would tell a teacher or a counselor that we did not feed her. Providers who saw her consistently noted, without prompting, that she did not look like a child who had missed meals. Her therapist heard about it so many times it became its own running thread in her case. None of that stopped the allegation from being made. It was not about food. It was never about food. It was about what the accusation of starvation produces: alarm, institutional attention, adults focused on us instead of on her.

The content of the allegation is almost always chosen strategically. She does not allege things at random. She alleges the things most likely to produce institutional response. Starvation. Physical abuse. Sexual abuse. These are not mild complaints. They are the allegations most likely to summon CPS, law enforcement, and school administration. And she has used all of them.

• • •

The broken arm incident sits in my memory with a quality of surreal exhaustion that has not faded. She had been in a major tantrum upstairs, in the bathroom, over something that started with flushing clothing down the toilet and lying about it. She was banging on the walls, scratching herself, completely out of control in the way that was already becoming familiar. I was standing in the doorway watching it unfold when she fell into the bathtub. She was not pushed. I was not near her.

What followed was the allegation: I had shoved her. I had been abusive. I had hit her. She reported this to school the next day with an addition: I had broken her arm.

CPS investigated. During the interview, the caseworker asked her to show them where her arm had been broken. She paused. She thought. She flung her arm up, extended it toward the investigator, and said: this one. Her arm was fine. No marks, no swelling, no injury of any kind. She had to search for an arm to hold up because the broken arm did not exist.

She chose an alarming allegation. She staged physical evidence when she could. When the evidence was not there, she produced one anyway, pointing to an uninjured arm as proof of a break. The investigation found nothing. We moved on.

What I did not understand then, and understand now, is that this is not something that gets better when the investigation is cleared. The cleared investigation is not a deterrent. It is a setback, not a lesson. The next allegation will come. It always comes.

• • •

There was the afternoon I was preparing to travel to my brother's funeral when CPS arrived at our home.

My brother had died in a motorcycle accident. I was trying to arrange travel, trying to hold myself together, trying to keep the household functional while managing grief in a house that does not easily accommodate grief. Riley had gone to school that morning with no visible injuries, having attended a therapy appointment that very morning, immediately before the bus arrived to pick her up. Sometime during the school day she developed a visible mark or bruise on her cheek and around her eye. She told a staff member that I had hit her and given her a black eye.

The school called CPS and reported it. They had an obligation to respond, and I understood that then and understand it now. A child reported abuse. That is exactly what staff are trained to do and what they should do. The part that cannot be separated from the understanding is what it cost on that particular day: an emergency CPS investigation, at our home, while I was preparing to travel to bury my brother.

The caseworker came to the house unannounced. I was just getting out of the shower as Shane told me that CPS was at our front door. They interviewed us, they interviewed every member of the household, they interviewed character witnesses, they reviewed the available information. She found no concerns. The injury was consistent with self-infliction, the timeline was inconsistent with parental abuse, and the history of allegations was not unknown to the system. She cleared the matter and drove away.

Before her car had left the neighborhood, Riley began to spiral.

She screamed and cussed and banged her own head into the staircase wall with enough force to cause structural damage. My sister walked into the house, to pick up work supplies, unaware of what was unfolding and Riley physically attacked her. She kicked our dog. She turned on me. She made explicit, named, detailed threats to kill every member of our household, to kill herself, to shoot everyone at school, to stab her teacher. She said all of these things while hitting herself and screaming, while we called the police and tried to keep people from being seriously hurt.

Six officers were dispatched to our home and stayed for nearly four hours. They were professional and they were limited. The situation was classified as a mental health crisis. A mental health evaluator was brought in. Riley was not initially considered acute enough for involuntary hospitalization, even with such extremes that had just taken place, and only after the evaluator spoke directly with me and understood the full scope of the day did the assessment change: Involuntarily Acute. Even then, no facility would take her. So she stayed home, the police gave her her nighttime medications and walked her up to her room, locking the door behind them.

I flew across the country for my brother's funeral the following day. The original trigger, the thing that had set the whole day in motion, was that Riley was angry I was leaving for an out-of-state trip. One she was not going on.

• • •

I described the backyard staging incident earlier in this book, because it belongs to the cameras chapter and the story of how I came to document everything. But it belongs here too, because it is the allegation I consider the most calculated of all the ones she has made. She took something I disclosed in a therapy session intended to build connection, something deeply personal, something that cost me to say, and she filed it away. Days later, she attempted to use it as the mechanism for a sexual abuse allegation against me.

That incident changed something in how I understood what I was dealing with. The other allegations, even the most serious ones, had the quality of impulsive weaponization: something goes wrong, she reaches for the nearest available accusation. The backyard incident was different. She had heard my disclosure, identified its value as a weapon, waited, and then deployed it at a moment of maximum utility. That is not impulsive. That is planned.

• • •

The allegations do not stay inside the family. They reach outward. And some of them are so elaborate, so detached from ordinary reality, that they require their own telling.

One afternoon Riley ran away. Not in the way that kids run away, in anger or in grief, but with a destination in mind. She ran away to meet her boyfriend, who was a serial killer who lived in our attic, so that they could travel together to the North Pole to live with Santa Claus and get married and have their baby she was pregnant with. That was the stated plan.

We were searching everywhere for her. We were on and off the phone with police, for close to an hour.

At some point two young women driving down the highway spotted her walking on the side of the road and picked her up. They drove her to the nearest fire station.

When the police called to say she had been found, I drove to pick her up. What I arrived to was an interrogation.

She had told the officers that she was scared to come home, that I was not safe. I stood outside a fire station and answered questions about my own fitness as a parent while my daughter sat inside, eating snacks and chatting with the firemen, having just run away to meet up with a serial killer who lived in our attic.

The officers were doing their job. But I also stood there long enough to be thoroughly questioned before they went back to her and she told them, in full detail, about the serial killer boyfriend and the North Pole and Santa Claus and the baby. At that point the nature of what they were dealing with became clearer. They called me back over and I took her home.

That was the real version of the incident. It was documented. The firefighters and officers who were present knew what had actually happened because Riley had told them herself, in full detail. There was no assault. There was no inappropriate contact of any kind. There was a child who had run away and been brought to safety and picked up by her parent after a period of questioning that was understandable under the circumstances. What there was, apparently, was material.

Almost two years later, the fire station and firemen came up again. This time at school. This time the story had changed entirely. Riley told other students and a school counselor that my sister had driven her to the fire station specifically to drop her off there, in an elaborate scheme of sex trafficking. That the firefighters had then taken turns holding her down and gang raping her. That she was now, two years later, pregnant as a result. And that I had found out about the pregnancy and was planning to kill her and the baby.

This allegation names my sister as a participant in a sexual assault on a child. It names specific firefighters as perpetrators of gang rape. It alleges a pregnancy. It alleges that I intend to commit multiple murders. Every element of it is false, every element is documented as false, and every element is the kind of allegation that, if believed, would result in serious criminal investigation of several named adults. It was stated to children at school. It was stated to a school counselor whose professional obligation required her to take it seriously. It circulated.

A child who is acting out does not construct a two-year retrospective gang rape allegation naming her aunt as a co-conspirator and her father as a would-be murderer. The original incident was documented. The people who were present know what happened. But an allegation like that, once it exists in a community, is not fully extinguished by documentation.

• • •

The reach of allegations extends to people who are barely present in her life at all. My father lives across the country. He has met Riley only a handful of times. He has no ongoing contact with her, no role in her daily life, no relationship to speak of. She accused him of threatening to lock her in a dog crate. Not a figure she lives with, not someone who disciplines her or sets limits on her. A man she has met a few times, targeted because he existed and was available as a name to use.

And then there are those who are a constant in her life.

She has accused my sister of hitting her. My sister, who has been in the house during escalations, who has tried to help, who was physically attacked and left with a bite mark on her wrist and bruises from being punched and kicked. Who was physically attacked again at a family gathering there. The person who was injured by Riley is the person Riley accused of hitting her.

She has accused my mother of threatening to beat her and kill her. My mother, who has watched her grandchildren for us, who has taken Riley on special outings, who buys her clothes and shoes and tries to have a grandmother-granddaughter relationship with her, who has been present for more incidents than I can count, who has herself been kicked and slapped by Riley. The woman who has had bruises on her thighs from being kicked is the woman Riley said threatened to beat and kill her.

And then there is Shane. I described him in an earlier chapter as the person who stays calm when I have run out of calm, the person who takes the next shift without being asked, the person who gives grace in a house where grace was scarce. All of that is true. He is also the person Riley has accused of starving her, of abusing her, of shoving her. A man who has gotten up in the middle of escalations, who has stood between her and injury to others, who has made her dinner on the nights when I was working or too depleted to be in the same room with her and brought it to her without comment. A man she has physically assaulted. That man. She has accused him of not feeding her. She has accused him of abuse. She has accused him of physical assault. He documents it the same way I do. He keeps going the same way I do. And he does not say much about it, which is consistent with who he is.

Her older brother has not been spared either. She has accused him of pushing her down the stairs. During one incident, she was standing at the top of the staircase mid-tantrum, alone, and fell. When the dust settled she told us, then later anyone who would listen, that he had shoved her. He was in his room on the other side of the house with his door closed when it happened. We know this because we were watching, because by then we watched everything. He is eighteen years old and he has grown up in a house where his sister has made allegations against him, where his name has been in CPS reports, where he learned early that being in the wrong place when something happened with his sister meant he could be accused of causing it. He has learned to disappear during escalations not just to protect himself from her violence, but to protect himself from what comes after.

The accusations reach deep, and affect the people who least deserve them, and those people absorb them and keep showing up.

• • •

These are the larger allegations. The ones worth naming because they carry enough weight to require institutional response or to circulate through a community. They exist inside a much broader and more constant current of smaller accusations, lies, and distortions that run through every single day. She tells teachers things that did not happen. She tells therapists things that did not happen. She tells caseworkers things that did not happen. She tells children at school things that did not happen. The larger allegations are the machine running at full capacity. The daily current is the machine idling, always on, always generating.

• • •

There is a different kind of damage that is harder to document because it does not produce a case number or an investigative report. It produces silence. Changed looks. Neighborhood children who used to knock on our door and then stopped.

Early on, before we understood the full shape of what we were dealing with, Riley went around the neighborhood and told the other children what she had allegedly done with her brothers. Told them the way someone might brag about a secret, like it was something to be proud of. She told the kids on our street, the ones who played with our oldest sons, that she had had sex with her brothers.

It was not true. There was a CPS investigation, and it was unsubstantiated. But the investigation happened, the story had been told, which meant the neighbors knew an investigation had happened, which meant the story had already moved through the street before anyone had any facts. Our oldest son lost friends over it. Not to a confrontation or an argument, but to that particular kind of social withdrawal where people just quietly stop showing up. Neighborhood kids who had been coming around stopped being allowed to come around. Adults who had waved from driveways started not quite meeting our eyes.

The investigation cleared. The allegation was false. Those facts did not travel as far or as fast as the allegation did, because that is how it works. An allegation moves outward immediately. The clearing of it moves quietly, if it moves at all. And our sons, who had done nothing, who were themselves victims of what their sister had said about them, lost pieces of their social world that did not fully come back.

That is the cost that does not show up in any of the documentation I have accumulated over the years. There is no incident report for a friendship that ended. There is no police report for a neighborhood that shifted. There is only our sons, carrying something they did not ask for and should not have had to carry.

She alleged that her third-grade teacher had locked her in a closet for an entire school day. That was the allegation that followed the Aubrey incident I described in the previous chapter: the teacher had named the shift, called out the change in Riley's presentation, and the allegation was the response. The teacher did not lock her in a closet. She had done nothing wrong. What she had done was see something, and name it, and the 'mean girl' did not like to be seen.

She has made allegations to school staff, to CPS, to law enforcement, and to community members. About community members, her teachers, her counselors, her grandparents, her parents, and her brothers. None have been substantiated. Every single one has been investigated, which means every single one has consumed institutional resources, imposed burden on the people accused, and created a temporary context in which we are the subject of scrutiny rather than the people raising the alarm.

I document everything. I have for years. Not because it feels like protection, but because without documentation, her word against ours is not a fair contest. A child's allegation of abuse carries enormous institutional weight, as it should. Children are frequently the least powerful people in an abusive situation and the systems designed to protect them are for the most part calibrated accordingly. What those systems are not well-designed to handle is a child whose illness includes the persistent, strategic production of false allegations as a method of control. The documentation feels like building a legal case against my own daughter. That is not what I set out to do when I became a parent. But it is what the situation requires.

• • •

There is a moment I need to put in this chapter because it belongs here, and because leaving it out would make this account dishonest.

She had been escalating since morning. By evening, the argument was about dinner: she claimed we had said she could not eat, which we had not said. I could see the allegation building in real time, could track the trajectory toward the statement she was going to make at school the next morning. And in the middle of it, exhausted and furious, I said something I should not have said. I told her that if she was going to keep accusing us of neglecting or abusing her, then we might as well give something real to get accused of.

I wrote it down that same night. I am including it here because this is a true account and it belongs in a true account. I am not a perfect parent. I have lost my composure in ways I am not proud of. I think every parent has done the same at some point or another. What I said was wrong. What I said was not abuse. It was not a threat that was carried out. But it was a failure nonetheless, and it was a failure produced by years of a machine grinding against the people in its path.

I am still here. I still wrote it down. That is what you do.

• • •

The allegation is not a symptom in isolation. It is a tool in a system. It is one component of a larger behavioral architecture that includes the staging of physical evidence, the timing of allegations to follow consequences, the targeting of the most alarming claim available, and the use of genuine institutional responses to produce outcomes she wants. That is not a child who is confused or distressed. That is a child who has mapped the system and is using it.

Understanding this has not made any of it easier to live with. It has not made the investigations less disruptive, or the accusations less exhausting, or the afternoon my sister walked into a house mid-crisis and got attacked any less frightening. It has not given me back the morning I was preparing for my brother's funeral, or the evenings I was trying to spend with my family. It has not given back the childhood my other children should have had, a childhood without constant chaos and fear.

What it has given me is accuracy. And accuracy, in a situation like ours, is the only ground that holds.

CHAPTER NINE

Violence and the People It Reaches

It was not a tantrum.

A tantrum is something children outgrow.

There were approximately forty people in the room when it started.

We were at my grandfather's property's annual gathering. My grandfather built all that he has, over a lifetime of hard work in construction, starting with nothing and working until the work produced something worth having.

His home looks like it belongs in a magazine, the kind of property you see in magazine spreads of Aspen: large, immaculate, every detail considered. The event was something he hosted every year: close family, extended family, business associates, bank owners, doctors, political candidates, people who had known each other for decades and people who had not. The kind of gathering where everyone is on their best behavior because the room demands it.

I had been looking forward to it. We all had.

Riley had been told to stay near me rather than wandering the room unsupervised, which was not an unusual instruction and which, that evening, was the trigger. She sat across from me in her chair, glaring through me the way she does when something has already been decided, when the gathering has begun and the only question is when. We waited for the remaining guests to arrive. The room filled. Everything seemed, for a few minutes, fine.

What followed lasted over two hours.

Out of nowhere Riley started yelling and cussing at my sister and threw a water bottle at her. My mother came over to intervene and Riley kicked her. When my sister stepped in, Riley began punching her in the head. I got between them, grabbed Riley, and carried her outside, the whole time she was screaming that we were abusing her. Once we were in the yard behind the building the aggression turned on me: she tripped me and punched me in the face. I have a prosthetic leg, and when she tripped me I went down hard, catching myself on my hand, the impact traveling through my hip and residual limb. I had a busted lip and a bruised hand and a hip that hurt for days after. My sister had a puncture wound on her wrist from Riley's fingernails, a sore neck and back, and bruising from being punched and kicked repeatedly. My mother had visible bruising on her upper thighs from being kicked.

Riley had no visible marks.

We stayed outside in the grass for the full two hours while she screamed and kicked rocks and threw boots and threatened to kill us and to kill herself. We could not go back in. We were trying to prevent further harm and disruption to the people still inside, trying to protect my grandfather's event from the chaos we were already standing in the middle of. The videos we recorded that night, gathered from several family members when it was physically safe enough to record, show her screaming, yelling, hitting, kicking, scratching, cussing, throwing out accusations that we were the ones hurting her while she was the only person in the frame making contact with anyone, including herself.

When it was finally over, it just stopped. She ate dinner. We drove home that night once things had calmed instead of staying like we had planned.

• • •

I have already written about the rages in an earlier chapter, and I want to be clear about the distinction. The rages are a phenomenon unto themselves: the escalation cycle, the re-escalation, the four-plus-hour episodes, the self-injury during the peak of them. What I am describing here is different. That gathering was not a rage in the way that chapter describes. This was targeted, directed, sequential violence against specific people. She identified who was intervening, shifted her focus, struck.

There is a difference between a child who is dysregulated and flailing and a child who is selecting her targets.

Both happen. Both have happened in our home and in public and in front of people who should not have had to witness either. But they are not the same thing, and understanding that they are not the same thing matters for anyone trying to understand what we are actually dealing with.

• • •

At school, the violence has followed the same pattern. During a class period, after being told she could not access a computer, Riley began escalating. She was asked to come to the hallway to calm down. She threw her chair back into the table, shoved the paraprofessional who was moving toward her, then kicked her teacher in the pelvis area with a full-extension kick. The teacher had recently had surgery. Riley knew this.

On her way into the hallway she punched the window, kicked the door, slammed the door into the teacher, and swung on her a second time, connecting with the teacher's shoulder. The teacher was hurt. The paraprofessional was hurt. Riley was suspended for the remainder of the semester.

I have reviewed the video footage from the school. I have received written statements from the staff who were present. I have read them many times because they contain observations that are important beyond the incident itself. The teacher described watching Riley's body change in the moments before the escalation tipped: rigid, focused, different from her usual presentation. The principal, reviewing the hallway video footage, documented the moment after the incident when Riley then grabbed the teacher's hands and her entire body appeared to ripple and relax into a sobbing hug, on the same teacher she had just attacked. The school counselor asked directly whether she was speaking with Riley during the event. The answer was no. The school counselor wrote that she knew she was not talking to the Riley who comes to school every day.

Those staff members were hurt in their professional setting while doing their jobs. They had done nothing wrong. It happened because something tipped, in the way things tip with Riley, and the people nearby bore the cost of it. What I want to say about them is that they are not abstractions in this account. They are people who were injured, and who kept coming back. People who continue to try to help.

• • •

The violence does not stay outside the home. Our middle son was pushed down the stairs by his sister. Not a shove in the heat of a physical altercation: she approached him from behind and used both hands at the top of a flight of stairs. He was not badly hurt, and I am grateful for that. Both older sons have been included in her allegations and CPS reports in ways they did nothing to deserve. Our youngest, who was three at the time, was almost pushed down those same stairs on a separate occasion and was stopped only because Riley noticed someone was watching.

The violence does not stay with the people it is aimed at. It moves into everyone who shares the house, and changes what they know how to be. I will write about my sons in full in a later chapter. What belongs here is only this: they have all been in the room. They have all paid a cost they did not choose and cannot return.

• • •

She has harmed animals throughout the years we have had her. Our dog has been kicked hard enough to be sent across the room, and now reacts aggressively toward Riley when Riley is upset. This is documented. She has injured ducks and chickens. She shoved a cat off the balcony of our second story. I include these things not for shock value but because harm to animals is a clinically recognized indicator in risk assessment, and because this is an account that is trying to be accurate, and accuracy requires it.

• • •

The title of this chapter is about reach. Violence reaches. It does not stay inside the event that produced it; it moves outward through the people who were present and keeps moving.

My sister does not come to the house the way she used to. She still helps. She still shows up when we need her. But something changed since Riley has made the allegations and attacked her. She does not say much about it. She is not the kind of person who makes her injuries into a narrative. But the difference is visible in the way she moves through our space now, the slight recalibration of proximity and readiness. That is what violence does to a person even after the physical damage heals.

My mother has been kicked, slapped, screamed at, accused of threatening to beat Riley, investigated by proxy. She still comes over. She still watches the kids when we need her. She still tries to have a grandmother-granddaughter relationship with the child who has hurt her and those she loves. I have watched her try, repeatedly and with genuine effort, and I have watched Riley use that effort as a tool the way she uses everything:

as leverage, as something to destabilize when destabilization is useful. My mother keeps trying anyway. That is its own kind of courage, and I want it in the record.

Shane has been hit, kicked, accused, falsely reported, and has gotten up and made dinner afterward. He has stood in the gap between Riley and injury to others more times than I can count. He carries it more quietly than I do. I do not know the full shape of what it costs him because he does not often say. What I know is what I observe: the baseline level of alertness that neither of us has been without in years, the particular tiredness that accumulates when your home is also a place you have to be ready in.

And then there is what it has done to me. I am depressed in a way that is clinical and persistent and different from the sadness I came into this knowing I might feel. I have anxiety that produces full panic attacks. I am in a state of constant fight-or-flight that does not resolve between incidents because there is no between. I have PTSD. There are days I do not want to get out of bed because I know what the day will ask of me. There are times I have thought about taking my other children and leaving, just going, finding somewhere that does not feel like this. I have nightmares. I have woken up from dreams of screaming my youngest son's name. I am still here. That is the thing I can say with certainty: I am still here, still trying, still showing up to a situation that has cost me things I did not know I had to give.

We have become isolated. From family, from friends, from the ordinary social life that most people maintain without thinking about it. No one wants to step into what follows us. The chaos is not contained to our house; it extends into every space we bring Riley into and into the spaces people imagine we might bring her into. We do not get invited to things the way we used to. People who care about us stay at a distance that is easy to understand and impossible to entirely close. It is a specific kind of loneliness, the kind that comes not from being unknown but from being known too well.

• • •

There is also the matter of who else has been in the room. The forty people who watched. The strangers in the truck stop parking lot years earlier, the first time I carried her out of a restaurant. The neighbors who have heard things through windows. The school classroom full of students who were present for the assault of their teacher.

Violence radiates.

It is witnessed by people who carry the image of it and do not know what to do with it. Some of them are sympathetic. Some of them are not. Some of them form conclusions about our family based on what they saw, and those conclusions travel.

I cannot control that. I have stopped trying to. What I can control is what I document, and what I say out loud, and whether this account is honest about the full cost of what has happened in and around our family over years. The cost is not only ours. It belongs to everyone whose path has intersected with hers, who has been in the room when something tipped, and who walked away changed.

• • •

The epigraph of this chapter says it was not a tantrum, and that a tantrum is something children outgrow. I want to be precise about what I mean by that, because I am not using it as a condemnation. I am using it as a clinical distinction.

The behaviors described in this chapter are not developmental. They are not the testing of limits by a child who is learning where the lines are. They are not explosions of frustration in a child who lacks the vocabulary to express distress. Some of what Riley does fits those descriptions, and I have tried to hold that complexity honestly in earlier chapters. But a kick to a teacher's pelvis with full extension, knowing that teacher had recently had surgery: that is targeted. A two-handed shove from the top of a staircase: that is targeted. A punch to an aunt's head in front of forty witnesses: that is targeted. These acts have objects. They have outcomes that are sought rather than accidentally produced. They are what they are, and the people they reach carry what they carry.

Understanding does not undo what happened. But it determines what we do next. And the direction taken, in every case I have described in this chapter, has been toward the next day, toward documentation, toward the still-open question of what care is available for a child like mine, and toward the people in our lives who have been hurt and have kept showing up anyway.

They deserve to be named, even if I cannot name them here. They know who they are.

CHAPTER TEN

What the Systems Give and What They Take

She told me the police won't do anything, and she was laughing.

Before Riley came to us, systems failed her. That is the true beginning of this story, and it is important to say it before saying anything else. The Department of Human Services had contact with her biological family before she was even born. Her biological parents had seventeen children. All seventeen were either removed, aged out, or imprisoned. The abuse and neglect that shaped Riley's nervous system, that wired her threat-detection permanently high, that produced every behavior I have described in the preceding chapters: that was permitted to continue for years, across multiple children, in a family known to the system, before anyone was removed. The failure that made Riley who she is was not invisible. It was documented, screened out and deferred.

I am not telling this part of the story to assign blame across decades. I am telling it because the chapter has a title, and the title is about what systems give and what they take, and to understand what they have taken from us it is necessary to understand what they failed to give Riley long before she was ours.

• • •

When Riley and her brothers came into our lives, we were in the transition process, still learning who she was, still operating inside what I have described elsewhere as cautious optimism. We had concerns. They were not vague or general concerns; they were specific observations about specific behaviors that were emerging during visits and early placement. We raised those concerns with the caseworkers involved in the adoption process.

What we were told, in substance, was this: it was all or nothing. The sibling group would be adopted together or not at all. The implication was clear: raise too many concerns, push too hard for answers or supports, and the placement falls apart. You lose all of them, not just the one you are worried about.

I do not know what a caseworker in that position is supposed to say, or what disclosure requirements applied, or what information about Riley's history was even in the file at that point. What I know is what we were told and what we were not told, and what the effect of that was. The effect was that we adopted a child whose needs we did not fully understand, without the supports that might have changed the trajectory, inside a system that presented the adoption as a binary choice and moved on.

The supports did not appear after the adoption either. The post-adoption landscape for families in our situation is not a landscape at all. It is a drop. You are handed a child with a documented history of severe trauma, a complex diagnostic profile, and needs that exceed what most families are equipped to manage, and then you are on your own. The therapy is outpatient. The medication management is outpatient. The crisis services, when they exist, are designed for acute episodes rather than the chronic, escalating, years-long situation we were actually in. There is no infrastructure for what we needed. There never was.

• • •

We have personally contacted more than twenty-eight facilities across multiple states looking for residential placement for Riley. Our private insurer case manager searched all fifty states over a three-month period. A separate case manager through Riley's state insurance conducted additional searches over another three-month period. The answer, from every facility that responded, was no.

The reasons given were variations on the same theme: her IQ is too low, her diagnoses are too complex, her behaviors are too severe, her violent history disqualifies her from their program.

These are the exact reasons she needs intensive residential care.

They are also the reasons every facility that has the word residential in its name will not take her. The system has built a category of child that it acknowledges needs the highest level of care available and then ensured that no such care exists for children who meet that description.

This is not a paperwork failure. It is not an administrative gap that could be closed with better coordination. It is a structural feature of how mental health care for children is organized in this country:

facilities are funded and staffed for patients who are manageable, and the children who are not manageable are sent back to the families that called for help in the first place. Every provider who has evaluated Riley has said some version of the same thing: she needs more than we can offer here. And then they close the file.

We have had multiple inpatient hospitalizations. Each one followed the same arc: acute stabilization in the inpatient setting, discharge without transitional residential placement, immediate decompensation at home, re-hospitalization. The cycle is not a mystery. It is not unpredictable. Every person involved in her care has watched it happen and expressed concern about it, and the discharge has proceeded anyway because there is nowhere else to send her and the insurance coverage has run out because she is no longer acute, and the bed is needed. Short-term stabilization without transition to appropriate long-term care is not treatment. It is a revolving door dressed up in clinical language.

• • •

Insurance should be its own chapter within this chapter. Imagine this: An acute inpatient hospitalization that was authorized in advance, approved by both her primary and secondary insurers, and completed with full documentation was subsequently denied retroactively as not medically necessary. Not medically necessary. A child who had threatened to kill her family, who had made explicit plans, who had been assessed by a mental health evaluator as meeting criteria for non-voluntary admission, who has acted on threats, who has physically assaulted numerous people, poisoned a parent, threatened to kill teachers at her school: not medically necessary.

I have spent hours on the phone and emailing with insurance case managers. I have submitted documentation, written letters, requested peer-to-peer reviews, navigated appeal processes designed to be exhausting. I understand that insurance is a business and that claims are evaluated against criteria that are themselves designed to minimize cost. I understand the mechanics. What I cannot absorb, no matter how clearly I understand the mechanics, is the application of cost-benefit logic to a fourteen-year-old child in psychiatric crisis and a family in imminent danger. The math the insurance company is doing is not the math of her or our safety. It is the math of their liability, and those are not the same calculation.

• • •

Law enforcement has been to our home multiple times. On the most significant occasion, six officers were dispatched and remained on scene for nearly four hours. They were professional. They were, within the limits of what their tools allow, genuinely trying to help. And they could do very little.

The legal framework governing mental health crises places significant constraints on what officers can do when the person in crisis is a minor and has not committed a qualifying criminal act. The threshold for intervention is high. The officers explained this to us directly, on our property, while Riley was still escalating inside. She has heard officers say this. She has processed what it means. The epigraph of this chapter is drawn from an actual moment: she stated, while I was on the phone discussing whether to call police, that the police won't do anything. She said it laughing. She was not wrong.

When the matter has been referred beyond the immediate crisis, the answer from the District Attorney's office has been consistent: this is a mental health issue, not a criminal one or her IQ prevents her from being competent. That framing is not inaccurate. Riley's behaviors are produced by illness, and the appropriate response to illness is treatment. The problem is that treatment, as I have described at length, is not available. The mental health system says she needs more than they can provide. The criminal justice system says it is a mental health matter. The insurance company says it is not medically necessary. The residential facilities say her profile disqualifies her. And she remains in our home.

• • •

There is a logic to how we arrived here, and it is not a complicated logic. A child suffered severe and documented abuse and neglect in a family known to the state. The state removed her too late and placed her without adequate disclosure or post-placement support. The trauma that was permitted to develop produced a psychiatric profile that now exceeds the capacity of every system designed to address it. Each system, encountering its own boundary, passes the problem to the next system.

The next system encounters its own boundary. The problem returns to the family.

We are the end of that circuit. Not because we are the right place for it to stop, but because we are the place where it stops when everywhere else has said no. Every official finding of no substantiation, every cleared CPS investigation, every insurance denial, every residential rejection letter is a document that says: not us. The accumulation of not us is the record of how we got here.

I want to be fair to the individuals within these systems, because I have encountered many people doing their jobs conscientiously inside structures that constrain what is possible. The police officers who came to our home were not indifferent. The CPS workers who investigated allegations in our home were not careless. The clinicians who evaluated Riley and said she needed higher care were telling the truth. The failure is not individual; it is architectural. It is built into how these systems are designed, funded, and bounded. Individual competence and individual compassion cannot fix a structural problem, and the structure of the mental health and child welfare systems in this country is not designed for children like Riley.

That is a polite way to say it. The less polite way is that children like Riley exist in a gap between systems, visible to all of them, helped adequately by none of them, and left with the families that took them in. Those families do the best they can until the best they can is no longer enough. We are at that point. We have been at that point for some time.

• • •

I did not write this chapter to absolve myself of responsibility for my daughter's care. I am her parent. The responsibility is mine and Shane's, and we have tried to meet it without flinching for years. What I wrote it to show is that the responsibility should not have been ours alone. That is the difference between accountability and abandonment, and what the systems have done, collectively and consistently, is abandon a child they created the conditions to harm, abandon the family that tried to repair that harm, and then document the failure with the language of necessity.

She laughed when she said the police won't do anything.

She is fourteen years old and she has already learned more about the limits of institutional response than most adults ever know. She learned it by testing those limits, one escalation at a time, and finding them exactly where the systems had placed them. That knowledge has not made her safer. It has made her more dangerous, because deterrence requires the credible possibility of consequence, and consequence requires a system willing to act, and the systems have shown her, repeatedly and consistently, that they are not.

We are still here. The systems are still not.

CHAPTER ELEVEN
Sleep and What Replaces It

Exhaustion of this kind does not feel like tiredness.
It feels like something leaving.

I do not sleep the way I used to sleep. I am not sure I remember what that was like, the kind of sleep that ends when your body decides it has had enough rather than when something outside you demands attention.

What I do now is closer to a suspension: a few hours of reduced consciousness during which some part of me remains online, calibrated, waiting. It is not rest in the way that the word implies repair. It is more like a pause.

Shane sleeps the same way. We have not discussed it much, because there is not much to discuss: it is simply what sleep is now, for both of us, and has been for long enough that we no longer have a clear memory of the alternative. You adjust. You do not choose to adjust; the adjustment happens to you, the way all adaptations to chronic stress happen, gradually and without announcement, until the new baseline feels like the only one that ever existed.

Before any of us goes to sleep there is a check: the doors, the locks, the sharps protocol, the location of anything that could be a weapon. It is not a checklist we write down. It is a sequence that has become automatic, the way any repeated action becomes automatic, the way parents of young children check the stove before bed. Except we are not checking for a stove. We are checking for our daughter.

• • •

Riley's relationship with nighttime has always been adversarial. The later the hour, the more agitated, the more provocative, the more inclined toward behaviors designed to prevent everyone in the household from resting. Evening, in the clinical documentation I have accumulated, is described as a high-risk period. In practice it means that the hours between four in the afternoon and midnight carry a particular quality of dread that is hard to describe to someone who has not lived inside it.

There are nights I end up staying up in the living room. I sit there in the dark with my phone and my laptop, sometimes documenting, sometimes just waiting for the house to go quiet in a way that feels settled rather than paused. Those nights are long in a way that daytime hours are not.

There have been nights when I did not sleep at all and went to work the next day and ran a business and came home and did it again.

There have been fewer of those nights during her hospitalizations, that have been the only periods in years when Shane and I have slept without a portion of our attention remaining on the door. The first night after an admission I always sleep badly, not from worry but from the strangeness of not being vigilant, the disorientation of a nervous system that has been running in threat-detection mode for so long that the absence of threat feels wrong. It takes a few nights to approximate rest. Then she comes home and it starts again.

• • •

Sleep deprivation, sustained over years, is not simply the absence of rest. It is an active process of degradation. The cognitive effects accumulate: reaction time slows, emotional regulation becomes harder, the capacity for complex problem-solving diminishes. Decisions that would have been clear become murky. Patience, which was never infinite, becomes a resource that runs out earlier in the day and replenishes less overnight. The person who shows up to the school meeting or the clinical appointment or the insurance appeal is a version of me operating significantly below the capacity I had when this started, and that capacity is what this situation most requires.

The body keeps its own account. My blood pressure is elevated in ways my doctor monitors with care. My cortisol is chronically high, stuck from prolonged trauma exposure: the body stops believing the danger will end and simply locks the emergency response in as its new resting state. My immune system is compromised. I am an amputee, and what chronic stress and sleep deprivation do to tissue health, to the interface between residual limb and prosthetic, to the daily management of a body that already requires more maintenance than an intact one, all of that is compounded by years of this. The costs show up at the doctor's office, in the mirror, in the way I move through a day.

What I have noticed, over years, is that the depletion changes not just how I function but what I feel. The emotional range narrows. Joy becomes harder to access, not because I am not glad of the things that are good, but because the channel between the experience and the feeling seems to have narrowed, as if the emotional bandwidth is being consumed by the sustained low-level emergency of daily life and there is not much left for anything else. I know this is a clinical description of what chronic stress does to affect regulation. Knowing what it is does not change what it is.

• • •

The chapter is titled Sleep and What Replaces It, and that second part deserves its own attention, because something does replace it. The question is what.

What replaces sleep, in a house like ours, is vigilance. It is the sustained attention that does not fully release even during the hours when it should. It is the part of the mind that runs background checks on sounds in the night, on the creak of a door, on a change in the quality of quiet that might mean something or might mean nothing. Vigilance is a survival adaptation that is very useful when the threat is real and very costly when it is sustained indefinitely. We are years into indefinite.

What else replaces sleep is the work that cannot be done during the day when managing Riley requires full presence. The documentation I write is often written between ten at night and two in the morning, in the windows between her finally settling and the household needing to be operational again. The emails to providers, the incident reports, the letters to insurance, the records requests, the letters to the school: much of this happens in the dark, in the particular quiet of a house that is temporarily not in crisis. That is the time I have, and it is the time those things require, and the cost of doing them is the sleep I am not getting.

What else replaces sleep is the conversation that Shane and I have learned to have in the margins of the day: the quick exchange in the morning before the house wakes up, the look across a room that carries a full assessment of the current situation, the debrief at the end of a day when both of us are too tired to speak in full sentences but need to establish what happened and what to watch for while the other goes to work. These conversations are our relationship now, in large part. We do not have the evenings. We have the margins. That is not a complaint exactly; it is a description of what intimacy looks like when it has been reorganized around crisis management. We are still here and we are still talking, which is something. But something is not the same as what we had before, and what we had before is not coming back until something in our situation changes, and the something that needs to change is not within our power to change alone.

• • •

I think about what this is doing over time. Not what it has done, which is considerable and documented, but what it is in the process of doing, the direction of the trajectory. A person can sustain a great deal if the end is visible. What is harder is sustaining it when there is no visible end, when the circumstances that produce the depletion show no sign of resolving, when the systems that might change those circumstances have repeatedly demonstrated that they will not. What that produces, over time, is not just exhaustion but something more fundamental: a change in the relationship between effort and belief. You keep doing the work because the work must be done and because the alternative is worse than the doing. But the belief that the doing will eventually produce something different becomes harder to maintain.

I am still maintaining it. Some days more than others. There are mornings when I wake up and for a moment, before the day's particular requirements have assembled themselves, it is just a morning. I have learned to stay in those moments. They are brief and they are real and they cost nothing, and in an accounting where everything costs something that is worth noting.

Shane has a saying he does not say out loud but that I can see in his eyes: one more day. Not in the sense of endurance, not as a gritted determination. More as an orientation. Today is the day we are in. Tomorrow is tomorrow's problem. It is a kind of temporal discipline that I have come to understand as one of the most adaptive things either of us has developed through all of this. Not looking at the full weight of what may still be ahead, but at what is in front of us right now, which is manageable, just barely, just enough.

We are tired in a way that goes below tired, down into something that does not have an ordinary name. We are also, still, here. Both of those things are true at the same time. I have stopped trying to resolve the contradiction and started treating it as simply the condition: depleted and present, exhausted and still moving, running on what is left and finding, so far, that what is left is enough for one more day.

CHAPTER TWELVE
What Professionals Don't See

The room you evaluate in is not the room I go home to.

She walks into a clinical office and becomes a different child. The mechanism is real and documented: Reactive Attachment Disorder produces children who present as charming and cooperative with strangers while reserving the full weight of their pathology for the people closest to them. Knowing this does not make sitting across from a clinician who has just spent forty-five minutes with her and is telling you how well she is doing any less disorienting.

She walks into a session and she performs. Not cynically, not with conscious calculation, though in some presentations I believe there is calculation involved. Something in her nervous system recognizes a stranger as safe in a way that I am not safe, and in that safety she becomes a version of herself that is easier to be around, more cooperative, more verbal, more apparently functional. She answers questions. She makes eye contact. She demonstrates, in the bounded context of a clinical hour, a level of engagement and responsiveness that bears almost no resemblance to the child who came home from that same appointment and spent the following three hours screaming and slamming her body into the walls.

I have sat in meetings with people who evaluated her and listened to their findings, and I have had to choose between two responses: accept what they observed as valid and wonder if I am the problem, or hold my own documentation against theirs and present the case for a different picture. I have always done the second. Not because I am certain I am right about everything, but because the documentation is not mine alone. The school staff see what I see. The extended family sees what I see. The police officers who have been to our home see what I see. The only people who consistently see something different are the ones who see her for an hour at a time in a quiet room with no stakes.

• • •

Therapy has been a particular site of this problem. Over the years Riley has had multiple therapists, and the pattern has been consistent with most of them regardless of the individual provider: she presents in session as more regulated, more reflective, more capable of insight than she is at any other time. This is not entirely without value. Something in the therapeutic relationship produces a version of her that is worth seeing, and I do not dismiss that.

I want to be specific here, because not every therapist has fit this pattern. Her RAD therapist has been different. She understands what she is seeing. She has not needed the documentation to believe the picture I am describing, because she has the clinical framework to understand why what she observes in session and what we describe at home are not contradictory. She does not need me to prove it. She already knows. That relationship has been the exception, and without it I am not certain we would still be standing. The rule, across most of the therapeutic relationships Riley has had, has been something else entirely.

The rule has been that the gap between what the therapist observes and what Shane and I observe becomes the subject of the therapy itself, in ways that are not useful. The question of why things are different at home invites explanations that center on the home environment. The home environment is examined. Recommendations are made about consistency, about consequences, about de-escalation strategies. All of these reflect genuine effort and genuine expertise. None of them account for the fact that the child in the therapy room and the child in our house are, in some meaningful clinical sense, not always the same person.

I have brought documentation to sessions: videos, incident reports, written statements from school staff. I have done this not to build a case against my daughter but because the gap between clinical observation and home reality was producing recommendations increasingly disconnected from what we were actually managing. A therapist who has watched Riley calmly discuss her feelings for fifty minutes cannot fully picture the same child slamming her head into windows two hours later. The video closes that gap. It does not close it completely, but it closes it enough that the conversation can be grounded in something other than the therapist's most recent session and my verbal description of what I went home to.

• • •

Formal evaluations present a different version of the same problem. Riley has undergone multiple comprehensive psychological evaluations, and the findings have been significant and important and have informed advocacy I could not have conducted without them. The evaluations are not the problem. The problem is what they cannot capture.

A psychological evaluation is a structured series of tasks administered in a controlled environment over a defined period. It measures what it measures under those conditions. What it cannot measure is the child at four in the afternoon when the school day has ended and the structure has released. It cannot measure the child at eleven at night when the household has been in escalation for three hours and there is no end visible. It cannot measure the shift in her eyes that multiple people have independently documented, the physical changes that accompany the state I have described throughout this book. The evaluation captures a profile. The profile is accurate as far as it goes. It does not go all the way home.

• • •

There is an experience that parents of children like Riley accumulate over years, and it is the experience of being disbelieved by the people whose job it is to believe them. Not disbelieved dramatically, not told directly that they are lying or exaggerating. Disbelieved quietly, through the way a clinician's face settles when you describe something that does not match what they observed, through the gentle reframing of a symptom into something more manageable, through the recommendation of a strategy that would work for a different child, delivered with the confident warmth of someone who has not been in your house at midnight.

I have an educational background that gives me clinical vocabulary. I can name what I am observing. I can cite diagnostic criteria. I can frame an incident report in language that forces a certain kind of engagement. I know how to make what I am saying legible to a professional audience. That has been an advantage, and I am aware that most parents in my situation do not have it. What I wonder about, regularly, is what happens to those parents. If my level of documentation and clinical fluency is what it takes to be taken somewhat seriously, and I still experience the moments I have just described, then what is the experience of a parent who does not have my background, who is watching the same things happen in their house and cannot frame it in language that the system recognizes.

The answer, based on what I know of how these situations unfold, is that those parents are not believed. Their children are undertreated. The gap between the clinical observation and the home reality swallows everything that falls into it, and what falls into it most often is the truth.

• • •

The inpatient hospitalizations have been the setting where this gap is most consequential. A child is admitted in acute crisis. The inpatient environment is structured, supervised, and stripped of the triggers that are endemic to home life. She stabilizes. The stabilization is real; it is not a performance, it is what happens when the threat level is reduced and the environment is controlled. The clinical team observes the stabilized child. Discharge planning proceeds on the basis of what they observe.

What the clinical team does not observe, because it occurs after discharge, is the decompensation. They do not see the first afternoon home. They do not see the escalation that begins within twenty-four hours of the return to the environment that produced the crisis in the first place. They do not see the look on our youngest son's face when the house shifts back into threat mode. They do not sit in the living room at midnight with their phone, waiting for a quality of quiet that might not come.

They have our reports of these things. And I believe the clinicians who have treated Riley are, individually, trying to act on those reports. The problem is that a report is not an experience, and the weight a person places on information they have received secondhand is not the same as the weight they place on something they have witnessed directly. Every discharge has proceeded on the basis of what was observed in the inpatient setting, not on the basis of what I have described happening at home. The home is the room they do not evaluate in. It is also the room we go home to.

• • •

There is a kind of expertise that accumulates over years of living with a child that no professional can acquire in any number of clinical hours. Not because the professionals are less intelligent or less trained, but because their training is not in this child, in this house, in the specific texture of what this particular situation is. I know the signs that precede a significant escalation better than anyone who has ever evaluated Riley. I know the difference between a bad afternoon and a night that is going to end at a psychiatric hospital. I know what it means when her eyes change and I know how long it has been since they changed in that particular way. I know things about my daughter that are not in any clinical record, because clinical records document what is observable in clinical settings, and the most important things I know about her were never observable there.

That expertise is almost never asked for in a way that treats it as expertise. I am asked for history. I am asked to complete rating scales. I am asked to describe behaviors in the context of the behaviors the clinician is already tracking. I am not often asked what I know that the record does not contain, or what I would need a clinician to understand that no evaluation has captured. When I offer that information without being asked, it is received as parent report, which carries a specific clinical weight that is lower than direct observation and lower than formal assessment. I understand why the system is structured this way. I understand that parent report is vulnerable to bias and distortion. I am also the person who has been in the room every time, and the record does not fully reflect what I have seen there.

• • •

This book is, in part, an attempt to close that gap. Not by replacing clinical documentation, which matters and which I have spent years producing, but by putting into words the texture of what clinical documentation cannot hold. The room you evaluate in is not the room I go home to. That is not a criticism of evaluation. It is a statement about the limits of what any structured observation can capture when the thing being observed only fully reveals itself in conditions that no one would choose to create and that no one can replicate in a clinical setting.

If you are a clinician reading this: the parent sitting across from you knows things you do not know. Not because they are more intelligent or more trained, but because they have been there every time, in the room that is not your room, in the hours you do not observe. The rating scales they completed, the incident reports they brought, the videos they offered: these are the surface of what they know. The rest of it lives in their body, in the particular alertness they carry, in the way they read the quality of a quiet house and know immediately whether it is safe. Treat what they tell you as data. Treat what they show you as evidence. And when there is a gap between what you observed and what they describe, consider the possibility that the gap is real, that you are seeing one version of their child, and that the version they go home to is something else entirely.

I am still trying to get someone to see that version. I have been trying for years. This book is the longest document I have produced in that effort, and I am not done.

CHAPTER THIRTEEN
The Other Children

They did not ask for this.
None of them asked for this.

They are not context. They are not collateral. They are people, whole and individual, and each of them arrived in my life already carrying more than any child should have to carry, long before Riley came home.

What Riley has cost them is real and I will not minimize it. But I want to start somewhere else. I want to start before her.

• • •

Our oldest son came to us in 2016 from a Level E group home. Level E is the highest level of residential placement available for children in the foster care system, a structured, institutional environment for kids whose behavioral and psychiatric needs exceed what any family setting has been able to manage. He had been there because he had nowhere else to go. His siblings had been returned to their biological abusers while he was placed for adoption, which means he was separated from the only people he knew in a world that had already given him very little reason to trust any of it, and then placed in one foster home after another, each of which lasted no longer than twenty-four hours before the placement disrupted.

Twenty-four hours. He could not stay in a home, any home, for longer than a single day before something would break down and someone would send him back.

He is autistic, high-functioning, which in practice means that his needs are real and significant and frequently invisible to people who meet him and conclude, because he is articulate and socially capable on the surface, that the label does not quite fit. What it means in a family setting is a particular kind of rigidity, a certain need for consistency and predictability, and a specific vulnerability to the chaos that another person's dysregulation introduces into an environment. He had spent years in settings that could not give him what he needed, failing placement after placement not because he was bad but because no one had figured out yet how to be what he needed.

We met him in 2016. We finalized his adoption in 2017. He has lived with us since before Riley came home, which means he has watched every year of what this book describes, from the beginning.

He is eighteen now. We have guardianship, because he is autistic and because the world requires that kind of formal arrangement when a child you love turns eighteen and still needs the scaffolding of family in ways that adulthood does not automatically provide. He is a young man who has a job and a room with a biometric lock and a way of moving through our house that is the product of years of reading a threat environment and learning its patterns.

He manages the way the rest of us manage. He complains about her to us, and he removes himself when it gets bad, and he keeps going. He disappears when Riley's gathering begins. He has learned to read the same signs the rest of us read: the eyes, the stillness, the quality of air in the room that changes before anything else does. In this house you learn to handle things or you do not survive the week, and he has learned to handle things. That is not a small thing. That is not resilience in the ordinary sense. It is the specific adaptation of someone who has spent years inside a threat environment and learned its patterns well enough to navigate them. He is remarkable. He also should not have had to become this particular kind of remarkable.

Recently he apologized to me. He apologized for asking me to adopt his sister.

I looked at him, shocked, and said what was true: I do not blame you for any of this, son. Then I turned around and went to my room and cried.

He was the child who made me make a promise. He was the boy whose face I watched at a roller skating rink when his siblings were together again, the boy I wrote about in the first chapter of this book because that moment was the version of this story that begins with hope. He asked us to bring her home. He asked because she was his sister and he loved her and he had been separated from her and he was a child who did not know what he was asking.

He knows now. And he apologized for it.

I have written a lot of things in this book. This is among the hardest.

• • •

Our middle son came to us from a Level E group home, as his older brother had before him. They were not there at the same time. When he came home, his siblings were already here, and that was its own quiet thing, understated in the way that the most significant things in our family tend to be.

He had been removed from his biological family, returned to them, to the people who had hurt him, and then removed again when the abuse continued and the system finally stopped pretending it would not. He had come through that cycle and landed, like his brother, at the top of the placement ladder, in the most restrictive environment available, having exhausted every lesser option.

He has fetal alcohol syndrome. He has a traumatic brain injury that resulted in intellectual disability. These are not peripheral facts about him, not conditions that exist alongside his life. They are the foundation of it, shaped before he was born and before he had any say in any of it. His biological mother drank while he was in the womb and then his abuser hurt his brain after he arrived, and the consequences of both of those things will be with him every day for the rest of his life.

He is sixteen now. He is the one who, in their biological family before any of them came to us, was Riley's protector. I have written that word in this book before and I will write it again here because it belongs in both places. He was a child, a small child, in a family that was doing terrible things to all of them, and he positioned himself between Riley and some portion of what was happening. He did not have the words for it. He did not have the conceptual framework for what he was doing or why. He just did it, because that is who he is at some level that predates language and memory and any of the things we think of as forming a person's character.

And now he is one of the people who needs to be protected, from her.

I do not know what to do with that sentence. I have carried it for a long time and I still do not know what to do with it.

Riley had pushed him down the stairs. He has been named in CPS reports he did nothing to deserve. He has watched her dismantle, piece by piece, the stability of the home and family he finally got. His way of handling it is to mostly ignore it, and to keep track of where everyone else is. He checks on his younger brother. He checks on us. He does not make a production of it. He just does it, which is, I think, the same instinct that made him a protector before he had words for what a protector was.

He is remarkable in ways that cost him. I carry that sentence like a stone.

• • •

Our youngest son arrived in our home medically fragile.

He had been shaken by his biological abuser, and shaken again while in the foster care system. Shaken babies sustain a specific kind of brain injury, caused by the violent acceleration and deceleration of the brain inside the skull, and the damage it produces is diffuse and lasting. His injury caused the epilepsy he has had since. It shaped the vulnerabilities he carried into our home. He was not a healthy infant handed to us to protect. He was malnourished, he was a child who had been hurt by the people who were supposed to keep him safe, and he arrived needing more than ordinary care.

He is seven now. He has been with us since he was eight months old. He has been in our home for his entire conscious life, which means that what is ordinary to him is what he has grown up inside, and what he has grown up inside is this.

He has a PTSD diagnosis. He has an anxiety diagnosis. These did not come from what happened to him before us. They came from Riley. From years of living in a house where the next escalation was always possible and sometimes imminent, from learning before he had words for it that certain sounds and certain silences meant danger, from growing up with a sister who is jealous of him, who has targeted him, who has attempted to push him down the stairs, who would hurt him if the opportunity arose. He sleeps in our room. He sleeps on a cot in our closet, behind a locked door that requires a fingerprint to open. Not because he does not have a room of his own. Because he is a target for Riley: she is jealous of him, she wants to hurt him, she tries to manipulate him when no one is watching. The two older boys have biometric locks on their bedroom doors as well. This is what safety looks like in our home. This is the prison we have built instead of the family we planned on building.

He is seven years old and he knows things about threat and safety and the way a house can change quality in an instant that no seven-year-old should know. He reads rooms. He reads people. He has mapped the patterns of escalation in our home with a completeness that is, depending on the moment, either remarkable or heartbreaking or both at the same time.

There was a morning, while Riley was inpatient, when I woke in a panic. I had slept through my alarm. My youngest was not in our room. The door was closed. I began screaming his name before I was fully awake.

As an amputee it takes me a moment to put on my leg, and there were seconds while I was putting on my prosthetic and calling for him that felt like the longest seconds I have experienced in my life. Our older sons heard the commotion and came out of their rooms. I eventually got to the living room door.

He was sitting in the recliner watching cartoons. Eating a fruit and grain bar. Completely calm.

He looked at me and said:

Dad, I'm okay.

Riley is not here.

Remember?

I'm safe.

She's not here.

I'm just watching some TV.

He was seven years old explaining to his panicking father that he had already calculated the threat level of the house based on his sister's location, and that it was safe, and that I could stand down.

A seven-year-old trying to reassure his father that he was safe because his sister was not in the house.

I stood in the doorway of my own living room and felt something I could not name then and cannot name now. It was not relief, though I was relieved. It was not grief exactly, though it was adjacent to grief. It was the feeling of understanding fully, in a single moment, what you have allowed your children's lives to become without intending to and without being able to stop it. What you have asked them to absorb without asking them. What they have learned because they had to learn it, because the alternative was to be unaware in a house where awareness was the only protection available.

What stays with me is the way he said it. Not frightened, not relieved, not performing calm for my benefit. He had already done the calculation. She was not here. Therefore he was safe. He said it the way you state a fact that does not require comment. That is what has become the baseline. That is what normal is to him now, and the abnormality of it is not visible from inside it.

• • •

There is a version of their lives I think about sometimes. The version where they came to us and found safety and nothing more was asked of them. The version where the thing that had been done to them before us was the hard part, and after that the arc bent upward, slowly and imperfectly, but upward. Children who had already survived so much, arriving in a house that could finally hold them, and allow them to heal.

That version exists for two of them, partially. They have healed in some ways and grown in ways I am proud of and become people I love past my capacity to describe it. The healing is real and I do not want to write over it.

But it is not the only story. They arrived carrying what their histories had given them, and then they lived for years inside what Riley's illness produced, and they absorbed that too. They are carrying both. The weight before us and the weight since. And none of it was what they signed up for. None of them asked for the biological family they were born into. None of them asked for the system that failed them before we found them. None of them asked to be brought into a home that turned out to contain this.

They are remarkable. Each one of them. They have also paid for that in currencies they should never have had to spend.

I am their father. I cannot give them back what was taken before us. I cannot undo what has happened since. What I can do is see it clearly, put it into the record, and refuse to let it be invisible.

They did not ask for this. None of them asked for this. And they showed up anyway, every day, in a house that asked too much of them, and they kept going.

That is who my sons are.

CHAPTER FOURTEEN
The Language of Survival

You learn to say we're managing, because what else would you say.

We're hanging in there. That is the phrase. It is the answer to how are things going and how is she doing and how are you holding up, and it is the answer because the answer it replaces would take too long and ask too much of the person who asked the question. We're hanging in there is a courtesy. It is a sentence designed to close a conversation rather than open one, and after years of practice it comes out smoothly, without hesitation, with just enough weight to signal that things are not easy without conveying the actual magnitude of what is not easy. It is the most functional lie I tell on a regular basis.

It is not entirely a lie. We are, technically, managing. The house is still standing. The other children are going to school. The business is running. Shane and I are still here. By the external metrics that the phrase implies, we are hanging in there. What the phrase does not carry is the cost at which we are hanging in there, the infrastructure required to maintain the appearance of managing, the things that have been given up or ground down or quietly abandoned so that managing can continue to be the accurate word. The phrase is load-bearing in a way that is not visible from the outside, and I have come to understand that the invisibility is part of its function.

• • •

Living in a situation like ours produces its own vocabulary. Not metaphorical language but a specific, functional set of terms that we use with each other and with the small number of people who have been inside our situation long enough to understand what the terms mean.

We say it's started. That means her eyes have changed, the quality of the room has shifted, and we are now in the period that precedes escalation. When one of us says that to the other we both know what it means: clear the room of the other kids if possible, reduce stimulation, do not issue any instructions or corrections, and position yourself for what is coming. That phrase does not exist in ordinary parenting language. We built it because we needed it, because the thing it describes needed a name that could be communicated quickly and without explanation.

We say the other one. That means Aubrey. We do not say Aubrey's name when we are communicating in real time during an escalation, because naming her can sometimes accelerate the shift or confirm a presence we are trying not to reward with attention. So we say the other one, and we both know what we mean, and the conversation moves on.

We say it's been a day. That means bad. It means the kind of night you are still processing at noon the next day. We say it's been okay. That does not mean good. It means the ordinary bad, the chronic low-level grind that has stopped registering as a crisis because it is not one, technically, which is a different thing from being fine. We text these phrases to each other sometimes when one of us is at work. They contain a full report. They require no explanation.

None of this language existed before Riley came to us. All of it was built to describe things that we could not have anticipated needing to describe. That is how survival vocabulary works: it accumulates in response to experience, filling gaps that ordinary language does not cover because ordinary experience does not require them to be covered.

• • •

There is also the language you use inside your own head, which is different from the language you use with other people and different again from the language you use in documentation. The internal language is the least edited version of what is actually happening, and it is not always kind.

I have thought things I will not write here, not because this account is dishonest but because some of what lives in the interior of a person surviving years of this is not intended for an audience, not even an honest one. What I will say is that the internal language has ranged from the clinical to the desperate, from precise analysis to the kind of raw exhaustion that does not have sentences attached to it, just weight. I have had thoughts that frightened me. I have talked myself back from places I did not want to be. I have used every tool I have, the clinical vocabulary, the documentation habit, the faith that the situation is survivable, to stay on the side of still going.

One of the things I say to myself, regularly, is: one more day. I borrowed it from Shane, or I absorbed it from watching him, and it has become part of my own internal equipment. Not as a minimization of what is ahead but as a narrowing of scope: today is the task. Tomorrow has not arrived yet and does not require anything of me right now. That reduction of the horizon is something I had to learn, because my natural inclination is to project forward, to see the trajectory and calculate the distance remaining, and the distance remaining in a situation like ours is not a helpful thing to calculate. The calculation produces despair. One more day produces the next hour.

• • •

There are things that the language available to me does not adequately hold. I have noticed this throughout the writing of this book: the places where I reach for a sentence and the sentence that comes back is not quite right, it is an approximation of something that exists at a level below language, in the body and the nervous system and the accumulated weight of years.

The closest I can come to naming some of these things is this: there is a grief in this situation that does not follow the ordinary flow of grief, because its object is still present. I grieve the child I hoped I was bringing home, and yet she is still here. I grieve the family I imagined we would be, and we are still here, still trying to be something like that family despite all evidence that the version I imagined is not available. I grieve the other children's childhoods in real time, while their childhoods are still happening, knowing that what they are experiencing is shaping them in ways I did not choose for them and cannot undo. Grief of this kind does not have a recognized name. It is not bereavement. It is not loss in the way that word is ordinarily used. It is something closer to watching something be taken incrementally, slowly enough that each individual removal seems survivable, but fast enough that the accumulation is devastating.

There is also something that does not have a name to attach to it: the specific quality of connection that exists between people who have been through something together that most people cannot imagine. Shane and I do not have to explain ourselves to each other. We do not have to contextualize what we are feeling or justify the level of our responses to things. We have been in the same rooms, at the same hours, with the same information, and the shorthand we have built is not only functional. It is also intimate in a way that is particular to shared extremity. I would not have chosen this. But I am thankful for that specific intimacy.

• • •

There is one more kind of language that belongs in this chapter: what I say to Riley.

The honest answer is that I do not say very much to her that is not functional. Dinner is ready. Get dressed. Time to go. The language between us is transactional now, built around instructions and logistics and the management of what is immediately in front of us. It was not always like this. Early on, before we understood the full shape of what we were dealing with, there was more. There was the ordinary talk of a parent and a child, the nothing-much conversation that builds familiarity and warmth over time. That register is mostly gone now. It eroded the way things erode under sustained pressure: gradually, without a single moment that marked the end of it, until one day I noticed it had been a long time since we had talked about anything that was not a need or a crisis or a consequence.

She does not say I love you. I do not say it either. I have thought about this, what it means that we have arrived here, what it says about the relationship and about me as a parent. What I have landed on is that the absence of those words is not the absence of the thing they name, at least not on my side completely. I am still here. I still show up every day to a situation that costs me things I did not know I had to give. Whatever that is, it is something. But it does not look like what I thought love between a parent and a child would look like, and the gap between what I imagined and what is actual is one of the quieter losses in this account.

What I do say to her, consistently and without exception, is her name. I say it when I need her attention. I say it when I am trying to reach her in the middle of an escalation, using it as an anchor, a way of calling the Riley I know back from whatever state she has moved into. I say it without warmth sometimes and with it other times, depending on what the moment requires. The name is the one piece of language that remains available in every register, and I use it accordingly. That is, I think, the most honest version of the language of survival between us: I still say her name. I have not stopped. Whatever else has been lost in the years of this, that has not.

• • •

We're hanging in there.

It is still the answer I give. It will probably still be the answer tomorrow. But I want it on record, somewhere, that what the phrase contains is not indifference or minimization or the settled acceptance of people who have made their peace with a situation. What it contains is years. What it contains is the work of every chapter in this book, compressed into two words that fit comfortably in a hallway conversation and carry, if you know what to listen for, everything that has not been said.

You learn to say it because it is the right size for the space you are given. You learn to say it because the alternative, the full answer, would require the person asking to stay, and most people cannot stay, and you have stopped requiring that of them. You learn to say it because it is true enough, and because true enough is sometimes the best that language can do.

We are hanging in there. We are still here. That is, on most days, just enough.

CHAPTER FIFTEEN
What Love Looks Like Here

Love, at its most stripped down, is the refusal to look away.

People ask me sometimes, in the careful way people ask things they are not sure they should ask, whether I still love her. I understand why they ask. I have described, in the preceding chapters, things that would test the limits of any feeling. The honest answer is yes. The more honest answer is that what I feel has been so reshaped by the years of this that I am not always sure the word still fits the thing it is supposed to name.

What I know is what love looks like in practice, in this house, on an ordinary day. It looks like showing up to her IEP meeting after a night when she screamed for three hours. It looks like filing the insurance appeal for the fourth time, in language precise enough that they cannot dismiss it. It looks like Shane making her dinner on the nights when I am too depleted to be in the same room with her and bringing it to her without comment. It looks like Shane getting up in the middle of an escalation and taking the next shift without being asked, and neither of us saying much about it afterward because there is nothing much to say.

It also looks like the things too ordinary to record. The meal prepared and carried to the table on nights when the household cannot be in the same space without risk. The clothing laid out because she is not managing her own. The hygiene routine prompted again, for the hundredth consecutive day, without expectation that she will maintain it and without any longer believing she will, because that window closed years ago, but doing it anyway because it is what she needs and we are the people who are here. This is not love as warmth or love as longing. This is love as stewardship: the daily, unglamorous work of keeping a person alive and functional inside a life they cannot fully manage on their own.

It looks like the locked cabinet in the kitchen. The knives are in there. The cleaning supplies, the scissors, the medications, the things that become weapons in a house where the threat is not from outside but from inside, from a child we brought home and are responsible for. I do this every night without resentment, most nights, because keeping her from harming herself or others is inseparable from caring for her, even when the two do not feel connected. Safety management is not a tender act. It does not feel like love when you are performing it. But it is what love requires here, and we perform it without interruption and without exception, and without expecting her to understand what it costs.

It looks like the supervision that does not fully stop. The background awareness we carry of where she is in the house, what she has access to, how long the quiet has lasted and what kind of quiet it is. The check before bed. The listening during the night. We do not do this because we want to. We do it because the other children are also in this house, and they have already paid enough for something that was never their fault, and keeping them safe and keeping her safe is sometimes the same act and sometimes not, and when it is not we do both anyway. That is the shape of this family from the inside. That is what love requires when it is responsible for everyone in the room.

It does not look like warmth, most of the time. It does not feel, on most days, like what I thought love between a parent and a child would feel like. What remains is something harder and quieter and more difficult to name. Not absence. Something that has been through too much to still look the way it started.

I am still here. That is the sentence I keep returning to, because it is the truest thing I can say about what love looks like in this house. I still show up to her appointments. I still fight her insurance company. I still make the calls and file the paperwork and we advocate inside systems that have repeatedly demonstrated they do not want to be advocated to. I do not do those things because they feel good. I do them because she is our daughter and they are what she needs.

If that is not love, I do not have a better word for it. If it is, then this is what it looks like here.

CHAPTER SIXTEEN
What the House Holds

Surviving something and being unharmed by it are not the same thing.

This is what the house holds.

It holds the years of escalations that ended and the hours that followed before the next one began. It holds the documentation: the incident reports, the videos, the letters to insurance companies and school administrators and the residential facilities that all said no. It holds the nights I sat in the dark with my phone waiting for a quality of quiet that might not come. It holds the morning my youngest son explained to me, calmly and carefully, that he had already calculated whether it was safe to watch cartoons based on his sister's location.

It holds the pink and gold room and the room it soon became. It holds the blanket I pulled back and the smell that reached me before my eyes understood what they were looking at. It holds the things she destroyed and the things we replaced and the things we eventually stopped replacing. It holds the mattress we threw away. It holds the waterproof one we put in its place.

It holds the Drano. It holds the six words she said when asked why. It holds the chemical burns that took two weeks to heal. The therapy session afterward and the fact that she went to school that same morning as if nothing had happened, because for her, nothing had.

It holds the allegations, every one of them. The cleared investigations. The caseworkers who drove away while she was already beginning to spiral. The morning I was preparing to bury my brother. The fire station story that circulated at school two years after the fact, grown into something monstrous and detailed and completely false, naming people I love. It holds the neighborhood that shifted without explanation, the friends our sons lost to a story that was never true.

It holds Aubrey. Whatever Aubrey is, wherever she came from, whatever she has planned that Riley does not know about or cannot access: she is in here too. Looking through my daughter's eyes. Planning in ways my daughter cannot. Waiting.

It holds Shane, who took the next shift without being asked and has not stopped taking it. Who has been hit and accused and falsely reported and made dinner afterward. Who carries it more quietly than I do and has never once, in all the years of this, suggested that what we are going through is more than he is willing to do.

It holds my sons. All three of them. What they arrived carrying before she ever came home, and what they have absorbed since. The oldest, who apologized to me for asking us to make a promise we kept. The middle one, who was her protector before he had words for the concept, who now needs protecting from her, who checks on his younger brother anyway, who just does it, the way he always has. The youngest, who has spent his entire conscious life in this house and knows it in his body the way children are not supposed to know things; as threat, as pattern, as the constant low hum of what might happen next.

• • •

It holds her.

I have tried to hold her honestly in these pages. Not as a monster and not as a victim, though she is in some ways both. As a child who was damaged before she had memory, before she could speak, before she had any say in what was being done to her or what it would make her. As a child who has done things I could not have imagined a child doing, and who carries diagnoses that explain the shape of those things without excusing them, and who is still, underneath all of it, my daughter. I do not always know what to do with that last part, but I carry it anyway.

The house holds all of the yelling, all of the screaming, all of the hours of escalation that built toward nothing and ended in the same exhausted silence. It holds the damage: the door frames we have replaced, the walls, the windows, the things we locked and the things that got broken anyway.

It holds the vigil of every night, the particular cost of sleeping with part of your mind still running, the tiredness that goes below tired into something that does not have an ordinary name. It holds the PTSD. The anxiety. The nightmares. The days I did not want to get out of bed because I already knew what the day would cost.

It holds the isolation. The way the chaos is not contained to our walls but extends outward into every space we bring her and into every space people imagine we might bring her. The friends who stopped calling. The invitations that stopped coming. The particular loneliness of being known too well by too few people, and not known at all by everyone else.

It holds the love. Whatever shape that has taken, however far it has been stretched from what I thought love between a parent and a child would look like, it is still here. The showing up. The phone calls to facilities that will not accept her. The insurance appeals filed at midnight in the dark. The name I still say when I am trying to reach her, using it as an anchor, a way of calling back the child I know from wherever she has gone.

• • •

The house holds the parent who is sitting in the dark right now with their phone, waiting. The one who has been told, gently or not so gently, that what they are describing cannot be what they are describing. The one who has documentation that no one reads the way it was written. The one who knows things about their child that are not in any clinical record and that cannot be conveyed in a forty-five minute session in a quiet office. This is for you. What is happening in your house is real. The reason no one believes you is not that you are wrong. It is that what you are describing is outside the frame of what most people allow themselves to understand.

The house holds the clinicians and the caseworkers and the insurance reviewers and the residential facility administrators who read a file and see a diagnosis profile and make a decision about a family they have never met. This is what that file does not contain. This is the room you do not evaluate in. It is also the room we go home to, every night, regardless of what your paperwork says.

What the house holds is everything I have described here, and more than I could write.

It holds what it has cost and what it has taken and what we have done with what was left.

It holds what's left of a family hanging in there as best we can.

And if she ever reads this: I see you. I saw you from the beginning. I saw the girl who put on that coat in the parking lot before she even made it inside, grinning, not caring that it was not quite cold enough to need it. I saw her standing in a doorway looking at a room we had built for her, and her face doing the thing I had hoped for.

I carried that girl into every hard year that followed. I am carrying her still.

That is the house. That is what it holds.

OPEN LETTERS

From the Room You Do Not Evaluate In

You have my file. Now here is what it does not contain.

These letters are addressed to the systems and the people inside them. They are not written in anger, though anger lives in them. They are written because I have spent years communicating through the channels each of you has provided; the intake forms, the rating scales, the appeal letters, the incident reports, the phone calls that route to voicemail, the portals that time out before I finish typing; and those channels have not been sufficient to convey what I need you to understand.

So I am saying it here.

In the open.

The way a person speaks when the official channels have been exhausted and the only option left is to say it plainly and let it stand.

• • •

To Her Doctors

You see her for fifteen minutes. Sometimes twenty, if the schedule allows it. You review her medication list, you ask how she is sleeping, you note her weight and her affect and her general presentation, and you make decisions that govern the chemistry of her brain on the basis of what you observe in those minutes.

I am not here to tell you that your observations are wrong. What you see in your exam room is real. She is calm there. She is cooperative. She answers your questions. She does not scream or slam her body into your walls or threaten to kill the people in your waiting room. What you observe is accurate, and I have never disputed that.

What I am asking you to hold alongside your observation is the possibility that it is incomplete. That a child with Reactive Attachment Disorder, by the very architecture of the disorder, presents differently to strangers than she does to the people she lives with. That the fifteen minutes you have with her is a controlled environment with no stakes, and that the environment she goes home to is neither controlled nor without stakes. That the calm child you are assessing was, twelve hours before your appointment, banging her head into a staircase wall with enough force to crack drywall, and will be again twelve hours after.

I bring documentation because I have learned that my words are not sufficient. I bring videos, incident reports, written statements from her school, because the gap between your exam room and my living room is a gap that language alone does not close. I am asking you to watch them. Not to review the summary. Not to scan the file note. To watch the footage, with sound, for the full duration of the episode. To see the child who lives in my house, not just the one who visits your office.

She needs more than medication management. She needs clinicians who understand that the child in the chair across from you and the child I bring home from your parking lot are not always the same person, and that treating only the version you observe leaves the version I live with untreated.

I am not asking you to take my word over your own clinical judgment. I am asking you to let my word into the room alongside it.

• • •

To Her Therapists

I know the therapy room is different from the living room. I know that is part of its design, that the contained and neutral space is supposed to allow a different kind of engagement. I understand the theory. I have studied it myself.

What I need you to understand is that the difference between what she shows you and what we manage at home is not evidence that we are the problem. It is evidence of the disorder. It is what Reactive Attachment Disorder looks like from the inside: a child who can perform regulation for a stranger, who can demonstrate insight for an audience of one, who can sit in your office and discuss her feelings with a composure that evaporates the moment she crosses our threshold. That discrepancy is not a mystery to be investigated. It is a symptom to be understood.

When you sit across from us and suggest de-escalation strategies, I do not dismiss your expertise. But I need you to know that we have tried every strategy you are about to name. We tried them years ago. We tried them again after that. We tried variations and adaptations and the versions recommended by other therapists who came before you. The strategies are designed for children whose nervous systems can be reached by external regulation. Our daughter's nervous system was wired before she had words, in conditions that none of us were present for, and the wiring does not respond to the tools in your standardized kit. That is not a criticism of the kit. It is a description of the child.

Some of you have been extraordinary. One of you, her RAD therapist, understood from the beginning what the rest of us were only learning to name. You did not need me to prove what I was describing because you already had the clinical framework to hold it. That relationship has been the exception, and it may have been the only thing that kept us standing.

If you are reading this and you are not her, I am asking you to consider what made her different: she believed the parents before she had observed the behavior herself, because she understood that the observation gap is not a flaw in the parents' reporting but a feature of the disorder.

Believe the parents. Even when your session went well.

Especially when your session went well.

Read that again.

• • •

To Her Evaluators

You carry a particular weight in this, because your decisions travel further and land harder than most. You are the ones who determine the diagnostic frame. You are the ones who write the evaluations that insurance companies use to approve or deny care. You are the ones whose clinical language becomes the language that follows my daughter through every system she touches for the rest of her life.

I am asking you to use that language carefully and completely.

When you evaluate her, you capture a profile. The profile is accurate as far as it goes. It documents her IQ. It documents her diagnoses. It documents her behavioral history as reported by us and observed by you. What it does not capture is the differential between presentations, the measurable cognitive shift that occurs when the alternate presentation is active, the planning and sequencing that should not be possible at a Full Scale IQ of 54, the handwriting that changes, the vocabulary that changes, the eyes that change in a way that every person who has spent significant time with her has independently documented.

I understand that the dissociative features are still under evaluation. I understand that diagnostic precision matters and that a premature label can do harm. But I also understand that the absence of a complete diagnostic picture produces treatment recommendations that do not account for the full scope of what is happening. A treatment plan that addresses Riley without addressing what happens when Aubrey is present is a treatment plan built for half of my daughter. The other half may very well be the one who put Drano in my coffee.

I am asking you to spend the hours it takes. Not the hours your schedule allows or your reimbursement justifies, but the hours the complexity of this child requires. I know that is an unreasonable ask inside the system you work in. I am making it anyway, because the alternative is another evaluation that captures a profile and misses the child, and we have had enough of those.

Write it all down. Every observation, every discrepancy, every thing that does not fit neatly into the existing framework. Write it down even if you do not yet know what to call it. What you document becomes the record, and the record is the only thing that follows her into the next room, the next facility, the next system that will decide what she needs.

• • •

To the Psychiatric Hospitals

You stabilize her. I want to begin there, because it matters and I do not want it lost in what follows. When she is admitted in acute crisis and the inpatient environment takes over, something happens that does not happen in my house: she calms. The structure holds her. The supervision is constant. The triggers that are endemic to home life are absent. She becomes the version of herself that your clinical team observes, and that version is real, and I do not dispute it.

What I dispute is the decision that follows.

You discharge her on the basis of what you observe. She is no longer acute. She is stable. She is ready for a lower level of care. I understand the clinical logic. I understand the bed is needed. I understand the insurance authorization has ended. I understand all of the mechanics of why the discharge happens when it happens.

What I am asking you to understand is what happens next. Within twenty-four hours of returning to the home environment, the environment that produced the crisis you just "stabilized", she decompensates. The escalation cycle begins again. The household returns to threat mode. And the cycle that brought her to you in the first place resumes, and we are back where we started, except now we are also carrying the weight of having briefly glimpsed what our home feels like without the crisis in it.

Short-term stabilization without transitional residential placement is not treatment. I have said this in other parts of this account, and I will say it again here because you are the ones who need to hear it most: what you are providing is a revolving door. You have named it stabilization. You have documented it as clinical progress. What it actually is, from where I am standing, is a cycle you know will repeat, proceeding as scheduled, because the system has provided you with nothing else to offer and no language to say so. Every clinician who has been involved in her care has acknowledged this. The discharge has proceeded anyway, every time, because there is no step-down facility that will accept her diagnostic profile and no insurance authorization that extends beyond the acute window.

I am not asking you to hold her indefinitely. I am asking you to stop discharging her into a home that you know, because I have told you and because the readmission pattern proves it, cannot safely sustain what you are sending back to it. If there is no appropriate placement available, then say that out loud, in the discharge paperwork, in language that the insurance company and the state cannot ignore. Document that you are discharging a child into a setting you have assessed as insufficient, not because it is clinically appropriate but because the system has provided no alternative.

Put it in the record. Make them read it. Because right now, every discharge note I have received reads as though a clinical decision was made, when what actually happened was that a structural failure was ratified and the family absorbed the cost.

• • •

To the Insurance Companies

You denied an inpatient hospitalization retroactively as not medically necessary.

I want to sit with that sentence for a moment before I say anything else, because I think the people who make these determinations may have lost contact with what those words actually mean when they reach the family on the other end of the letter.

The hospitalization was authorized in advance. It was approved by both her primary and secondary insurers. She was admitted because she had threatened to kill her family, had made explicit plans, had been assessed by a licensed mental health evaluator as meeting criteria for involuntary admission, had a documented history of acting on threats of precisely this nature, and had physically assaulted multiple people. The admission met every clinical threshold your own criteria require. And then, afterward, from an office somewhere, having never met my daughter and never stood in my house and never had to calculate whether it was safe to go to sleep, someone decided it was not medically necessary.

I have spent hours on your phone lines. I have submitted documentation that I compiled at midnight in my living room after the household had finally settled, in the only window of time my day allows for the work your appeals process demands. I have written letters in clinical language precise enough that they cannot be dismissed, because I have learned that imprecise language gives you a chance to decline and you take every chance you are given. I have requested emergency appeals, I have requested peer-to-peer reviews with physicians who have never treated my child and whose role in the conversation is to apply cost-containment criteria to a clinical picture they encountered twenty minutes before the call.

I understand that you are a business. I understand that claims are evaluated against medical necessity criteria. I understand the mechanics. What I cannot absorb, no matter how thoroughly I understand the mechanics, is the application of cost-benefit logic to a fourteen-year-old in psychiatric crisis whose family is in physical danger. The math you are doing is not the math of her safety. It is not the math of my safety, my husband's safety, or my sons' safety, or the safety of the teachers and staff, or extended family members who see her every day. It is the math of your liability exposure, and you have decided that the liability of denial is less than the cost of authorization, and you are correct about that, because the cost of denial is absorbed by us. We are the line item you have decided not to fund.

Every appeal I file is a document that says: this child needed care and you refused to pay for it. I will keep filing them. I will keep writing them at midnight. And I want every reviewer who reads the next one to understand what the file on their screen represents: a family sitting in a locked down house, managing a crisis that your company has decided is not medically necessary, with children sleeping behind biometric locks because the alternative is not safe, doing the work your denial letter has made exclusively ours.

• • •

To the Department of Human Services

You knew about her biological family before she was born. The contact was documented. The abuse and neglect that produced every behavior described in this book was not invisible to you. It was in your files, in your screening records, in the reports that were received and assessed and, for years, deferred. Seventeen children. All seventeen removed, aged out, or incarcerated. The intervention that might have changed the trajectory of my daughter's life was within your power, and it came too late, after the damage had been done to a brain that was still forming and could not protect itself from what was happening to it.

I am not assigning blame across decades. The individuals who work within your agency are, in my experience, frequently competent and frequently constrained. What I am describing is a structural issue. The structure you operate within permitted the harm that made my daughter who she is, and then handed her to us without adequate disclosure, without adequate support, and without adequate follow-through.

When we raised concerns during the adoption process, we were told it was all or nothing. The sibling group together or not at all. The message was clear: ask too many questions, push too hard for information about what we were taking on, and the placement collapses and we lose all of them. That is not informed consent. That is coercion dressed as policy. We adopted a child whose needs exceeded anything we were told to expect, inside a system that presented the decision as binary and then moved on.

The post-adoption supports did not appear. They did not appear because they do not exist, and especially not at the level required for a child like ours. The therapy is outpatient. The crisis services are designed for acute episodes, not for the chronic, years-long, escalating situation we actually live in. There is no infrastructure for what we need. There never has been. You placed a child with a documented history of severe trauma into a family, and then you left that family to manage the consequences alone, and when the consequences exceeded what any family can manage, you had no next step to offer because the next step does not exist in your system.

I want to tell you what your system has produced. It has produced a family with biometric locks on bedroom doors. It has produced a seven-year-old who sleeps on a cot in his parents' closet because his sister is a danger to him. It has produced an eighteen-year-old who apologized to his father for asking us to adopt the sibling we told him we would bring home. It has produced parents with PTSD, panic attacks, chronic stress injuries, and a level of depletion that your intake forms do not have a field for.

You owe these families more than you are giving them. Not because they are fragile, but because the children you place with them are carrying damage that your system permitted, and the families that take those children on are doing the work that your system could not do and has not funded anyone else to do. The least you owe them is the truth about what they are taking on, and the support to survive it.

• • •

To Congress

There is a child in my home who every system acknowledges needs the highest level of psychiatric residential care available. Every clinician who has evaluated her has said some version of the same thing: she needs more than outpatient services can provide. Every inpatient facility that has treated her has discharged her with the recommendation for a transitional residential placement. We have contacted more than twenty-eight facilities across multiple states. Our private insurer searched all fifty states over a three-month period. Her state insurer conducted a separate search over another three months. The answer, from every facility, was no.

The reasons were always the same: her IQ is too low, her diagnoses are too complex, her behaviors are too severe, her history of violence disqualifies her. These are the exact reasons she needs residential care. They are also the reasons no residential facility in this country will take her.

You have built a system that creates a category of child it acknowledges cannot be served and then provides no mechanism for serving them. The mental health system says she needs more than it can offer. The criminal justice system says it is a mental health matter. The insurance company says it is not medically necessary. The residential facilities say her profile disqualifies her. And the child remains in the home, with a family that has been asking for help for years, absorbing a cost that no family should be asked to absorb alone.

This is not a gap. A gap implies that two structures were built with good intentions and did not quite meet in the middle. What I am describing is an absence. There is no structure. There is no residential option for the most severely affected children in the child welfare and psychiatric systems. There is no transitional care framework. There is no step-down protocol that bridges inpatient stabilization and home placement. There is a revolving door between the emergency room and the family, and the family is expected to function as a psychiatric residential facility without the staffing, the funding, the clinical oversight, or the shift changes that such a facility would require.

I am asking you to fund what does not exist. Not to study it. Not to commission a report about the feasibility of studying it. To fund it. Residential treatment capacity for children with complex diagnostic profiles—Reactive Attachment Disorder, intellectual disability, dissociative features, histories of violence—who are currently falling through every system because no system was designed to hold them.

I am also asking you to fund the families. The post-adoption support infrastructure is nonexistent, and especially at the level of need my family represents. Adoption subsidies do not cover the cost of biometric locks, waterproof mattresses, replacement door frames, or the lost income from a parent who cannot maintain full-time employment because someone must be home and vigilant at all times. They do not cover the therapy my other children need because of what they have lived through. They do not cover the medical costs of chronic stress on bodies that were already compromised.

You passed laws that moved children out of institutions and into families. That was the right thing to do for many children. But you did not build the support system that those families need when the child's needs exceed what a family setting can provide, and the absence of that support system is not a policy debate to the people living inside it. It is Tuesday. It is 1:56 in the morning.

And I am sitting in my living room writing this letter because my daughter is asleep and this is the only time I have, and tomorrow I will get up and do it again, and the day after that, and the day after that, for as long as the systems you oversee continue to provide nothing else.

• • •

To the Police

You have been to my home. Some of you have been there more than once. You have stood in my yard and my living room and listened to what was happening and tried, within the limits of what your tools allow, to help. I want to start with that, because it is true and because what follows is not about the individual officers who have responded to my calls. It is about what you are able to do when you arrive, and what you are not.

You arrived once, six of you, and stayed for nearly four hours. You were professional. You were patient. You managed a situation that was dangerous and chaotic with a steadiness that I appreciated at the time and have thought about since. And you could do very little. The legal framework governing mental health crises in minors placed constraints on your intervention that you explained to me directly, in my own yard, while my daughter was escalating inside.

She heard you explain it. She processed what it meant. She has since told me, laughing, that the police will not do anything. She was not wrong. She is fourteen years old and she has already mapped the limits of institutional response more thoroughly than most adults ever need to, and she has mapped them because she tested them and found them exactly where you placed them.

I do not blame you for the limits. You did not set them. But I need you to understand what the limits produce. They produce a child who knows that the consequences available to her parents are finite and that the system behind those consequences has a ceiling she has already reached. Deterrence requires the credible possibility of consequence. When that possibility has been tested and found absent, what remains is a household managing a level of threat that would be classified as criminal in any other relational context, with no external mechanism of accountability.

When I specifically asked what it was going to take to get help for this child, what she would actually have to do, you answered without hesitation. Unfortunately yes, you said. She would have to actually kill someone. Think about that for a moment.

Think about that for a moment.

When you respond to the next call from a house like mine, I am asking you to consider a few things. First:

the parent on the phone has already exhausted everything they have before they called you.

The call is not the beginning of the crisis. It is the end of a sequence that started hours or days before and has passed through every intervention available to us before arriving at your dispatch number. Second: the child you encounter when you arrive may not be the child who was present during the crisis. She may have shifted. She may be calm, cooperative, and charming in a way that makes the parent's description of what just happened difficult to credit. That shift is a feature of the disorder, not evidence that the parent exaggerated the event. Third: when the mental health evaluator determines that the child is not acute enough for involuntary hold, and you walk back to your car, the family is still in the house. They are still there after you leave. They will be there tomorrow. The crisis does not resolve when you clear the call.

I have called because I needed help. What I received was a professional and compassionate presence that could not do the thing I needed done, and then a departure. I understand why. I am asking you to advocate, within your departments and your unions and your policy channels, for the thing that is missing: a protocol for chronic, repeated mental health crises in minors that does not require the child to meet the threshold for involuntary commitment before any meaningful intervention is available. Because by the time that threshold is met, someone in the house has usually already been hurt. And the threshold, as your officers have explained to me on my own property, is very high. Higher than a punch. Higher than a kick to a teacher. Higher than Drano in a cup of coffee. The threshold is higher than what most people would accept as reasonable, and the people who live below it are the ones absorbing the cost of its position.

You cannot fix this. I know that. But you can stop leaving houses like mine with the impression that the situation has been resolved, because it has not. What has been resolved is the call. The situation continues after you leave. It continues tonight and tomorrow and next week, and the family you visited will call again, not because they want to, but because there is nothing else left to try, and calling you is the last available action before the only alternative is giving up entirely.

We have not given up. We are still calling. I am asking you to still come.

• • •

To the Schools

I want to begin with what you got right. Some of you did, and I need that acknowledged before anything else, because this letter is not only about what was missed.

Your third-grade teacher saw something in the first year and named it before we had words for it ourselves. When she looked at the child in front of her and said: I want to talk to Riley, that teacher did something that took real steadiness. She did not file it under difficult child and move on. She saw it clearly and she named it, and the allegation that followed the next morning, the one that accused her of locking Riley in a closet for an entire school day, was the direct result of her having been seen by something that does not like to be seen. That teacher came back. She kept teaching. I want that in the record.

Your school counselor sat across from my daughter in the middle of an escalation and knew with certainty that she was not talking to Riley. She wrote it down: I knew I was not talking to the Riley who comes to school every day. That is a significant clinical observation, made in real time, by someone who was paying close enough attention to see it. It mattered. It still matters.

Your paraprofessional and your teacher were hurt in their professional setting, doing their jobs, on an ordinary school day. Both were hurt. Both came back. They are not lost to this account. They are people who absorbed something they should never have had to absorb and returned to the same room because that is who they are. If they read this: I see what it cost you. I have not forgotten it.

I am naming what you got right because I need to be honest about what you did not, and that accounting requires the other side to exist first.

In the early years, when we were still trying to build a picture of what was happening and needed to be believed, the communications we received from school often reflected what Riley presented in your building: cooperative, plausible, charming. She is doing fine here was the message, offered by people who were not wrong about what they observed and who were not yet equipped to understand that what they observed was one version of a child with more than one. The home environment became the variable under examination. We were asked, in ways that ranged from gentle to less so, whether we had considered what in the home might be contributing to the behaviors we were describing. We had. The answer was not what anyone was suggesting it was.

Some of you received allegations from her that you were required to act on, and that is correct. A child reports something serious and the staff who hear it have an obligation. I understand that and I have never disputed it. What I am asking you to understand is what happens when that allegation circulates through a school hallway before anyone has established whether it is true. Our sons were in your buildings. They had done nothing. They were themselves being harmed by their sister. And they lost parts of their social world because stories travel faster in a school than facts do, and the clearing of an allegation does not move through hallways the way the allegation did. That cost was real and it did not come back.

The IEP process deserves its own accounting. The IEP is the document that is supposed to ensure what happens at school is adequate for the actual child, not the child who presents well in the observation window. I have brought documentation to those meetings: video, written statements from clinical providers, incident reports. Some of it was taken seriously. Much of it was received as parent report, which in practice meant it was noted and substantially discounted. The gap between what your building sees and what I go home to is the same gap I describe throughout this book. It exists in your setting as reliably as it exists anywhere else.

What I am asking is the same thing I ask every system in these letters, and it is not complicated: hold both pictures at once. The child who sits in your classroom and cooperates and charms and makes your staff feel like things are manageable, and the child I bring home from your parking lot who three hours later is slamming her body into the walls. They are the same child. Your staff have seen the shift with their own eyes. They have documented it independently and without coordinating with each other or with me. That convergence is not coincidence. It is the disorder, visible in a setting with enough structure to make the contrast legible.

Believe the parents who are describing something you have not seen in your building. Especially when your building is having a good week.

I am not asking you to be a psychiatric facility. I am asking you to be a school that takes seriously the possibility that a child can be two things at once: functional in a structured environment and genuinely, severely unsafe everywhere else. The structure of your building is part of what holds her together during the hours she is in it. I am grateful for that, genuinely. The moment she leaves it, the holding stops. The family she comes home to is the place where the structure releases, and we have been managing what releases without adequate support for years. Knowing that your building is one of the things that holds her, and that this is not nothing, does not close the gap. But it matters. And the staff who hold that structure, who show up every day to a student who has hurt them and might again, and who keep paying attention anyway: they are part of how this child has survived the years she has survived. I want them to know that I know it.

• • •

Still Here

These letters are addressed to systems, but they are read by people. If you are a person inside one of these systems, and you have read this far, then you have done something that most of the systems you work in do not: you have stayed with a story long enough to see its full shape. That is all I have ever asked. Not agreement. Not absolution. Just the willingness to hold the full picture and let it change what you do next.

I am not done advocating. I am not done documenting. I am not done showing up to the meetings and writing the letters and filing the appeals and making the calls.

I am still here.

I have always been here.

The question I leave with each of you is whether you will be.

www.ingramcontent.com/pod-product-compliance
Ingram Content Group UK Ltd.
Pitfield, Milton Keynes, MK11 3LW, UK
UKHW062311290726
14090UKWH00018B/999